In this book my friend Artie Davis cuts through the clutter of attractional, missional, and incarnational and focuses in on the key issue of the Christian life: Do we reflect the craveable life of Christ? Artie goes beyond theory and puts practical skin on the bones of what it means to live out the craveable life we were all created to live.

—GEOFF SURRATT
MANAGING DIRECTOR, EXPONENTIAL

Artie Davis, a rather craveable man, has written an excellent book about a much-needed subject—how to be more like Jesus. This book is a movement-maker, and the people to whom you pass it along will be equipped and challenged to turn their world upside down with a contagious lifestyle. So read it and buy copies for your friends. We need a movement of craveable Jesus-followers!

—BRANDON COX
LEAD PASTOR, GRACE HILLS CHURCH, ROGERS, AR
EDITOR AND COMMUNITY FACILITATOR, PASTORS.COM

Artie's mission matrix in *Craveable* is pure genius in its simplicity. No matter the missional context or size of your church—*Craveable* beautifully describes "what" God wants you and the people you lead to be in your missional context. The "how" is the unique fingerprint of God on your church and your community. That is left for you and your church to discover. I love *Craveable*.

—DERWIN L. GRAY
LEAD PASTOR, TRANSFORMATION CHURCH

In *Craveable* Artie takes us back two thousand years and gives us a glimpse into what the New Testament church looked like— something that everyone wanted to be a part of. *Craveable* is definitely a book that every Christ-follower must read!

—SHAWN LOVEJOY
SENIOR PASTOR, MOUNTAIN LAKE CHURCH, AND AUTHOR OF *THE MEASURE OF OUR SUCCESS: AN IMPASSIONED PLEA TO PASTORS*

One of the biggest problems facing the church today is that the people around us just don't seem interested in what we are offering. My friend Artie Davis thinks things should be different. His new book, *Craveable*, will help you understand the power of living a life that makes those around you want what you have.

—GREG SURRATT
LEAD PASTOR, SEACOAST CHURCH, AND AUTHOR OF *IR-REV-REND*

It's been said, "People are more influenced by the sermons that you live than the ones that you preach." Artie's new book, *Craveable*, brings this concept to life. *Craveable* is a practical handbook for Christians, challenging us to truly help those we come in contact with by demonstrating how they can find, follow, and be like Jesus. If you want the irresistible light of Jesus to shine from the inside out, read *Craveable*.

—SCOTT WILLIAMS
AUTHOR OF *CHURCH DIVERSITY* AND *GO BIG*
CEO, NXT LEVEL SOLUTIONS

CRAVE
ABLE

CRAVE
ABLE

ARTIE DAVIS

PASSIO

Most CHARISMA HOUSE BOOK GROUP products are available at special quantity discounts for bulk purchase for sales promotions, premiums, fund-raising, and educational needs. For details, write Charisma House Book Group, 600 Rinehart Road, Lake Mary, Florida 32746, or telephone (407) 333-0600.

CRAVEABLE by Artie Davis
Published by Passio
Charisma Media/Charisma House Book Group
600 Rinehart Road
Lake Mary, Florida 32746
www.charismahouse.com

Unless otherwise noted, all Scripture quotations are from the New King James Version of the Bible. Copyright © 1979, 1980, 1982 by Thomas Nelson, Inc., publishers. Used by permission.

Scripture quotations marked CEV are from the Contemporary English Version, copyright © 1995 by the American Bible Society. Used by permission.

Scripture quotations marked ERV are from the Easy-to-Read Version, copyright © 2006 by World Bible Translation Center. Used by permission.

Scripture quotations marked ESV are from the Holy Bible, English Standard Version. Copyright © 2001 by Crossway Bibles, a division of Good News Publishers. Used by permission.

Scripture quotations marked GNT are from the Good News Translation. Copyright © 1992 by American Bible Society. Used by permission.

Scripture quotations marked GW are from GOD'S WORD Translation. Copyright © 1995 by God's Word to the Nations. Used by permission of Baker Publishing Group.

Scripture quotations marked HCSB are from the Holman Christian Standard Bible. Copyright © 1999, 2000, 2002, 2003 by Holman Bible Publishers, Nashville, Tennessee. All rights reserved. Used by permission.

Copyright © 2013 by Artie Davis
All rights reserved

Cover design by Lisa Cox
Design Director: Bill Johnson

Visit the author's website at www.artiedavis.com.

Library of Congress Control Number: 2012918796
International Standard Book Number: 978-1-61638-970-3
E-book ISBN: 978-1-61638-971-0

While the author has made every effort to provide accurate telephone numbers and Internet addresses at the time of publication, neither the publisher nor the author assumes any responsibility for errors or for changes that occur after publication.

First edition

13 14 15 16 17 — 9 8 7 6 5 4 3 2 1
Printed in the United States of America

This book is dedicated to those who have written it for me; those who have loved me, taught me, and corrected me; those who have suffered with me during times of great defeat and fought for me in times of great victory:

To my incredible wife, Georgie, and my kids: Rebecca and Tim, Leah, Paul-Henry, and Markia Randal.

To my parents, sisters, church, staff, and friends.

They have all been a part of creating this book. I am incredibly blessed to have such people in my life.

CONTENTS

Part 2: Craveable Listening

Part 3: Craveable Looking

Part 4: Craveable Loving

Part 5: Craveable Living

Part 6: Craveable Learning

Part 7: Craveable Leading

Part 8: Craveable Leaving

Part 9: Craveable Us

FOREWORD

WHEN I WAS in the sixth grade, I had a group of rowdy friends. Of course, rowdy for sixth graders thirty-five years ago probably had a different meaning than it would have today. For me, it meant we were disrespectful of our teachers at times and obnoxious to other students...especially girls. I wanted to be just like them. They were hip, cool, groovy...whatever the word was in that day. (I don't remember.)

One day one of my teachers pulled me aside and said something that even today proves to have been a life-changing encouragement. She said, "Ron, I know your family, and those boys don't have the same upbringing you have had. If you keep hanging out with that crowd, you're going to eventually end up where they do, and I promise you that's not where you want to be someday."

I didn't know all that meant, but it was enough to help me choose a different set of friends as I entered the seventh grade. Looking back, the path of my life compared to the path I know of several of those sixth-grade friends is miles apart. I'm so thankful for that word of encouragement. (By the way, I have told that teacher the impact she had on my life.)

Fast-forward twenty years. I was then a young father. My boys were elementary aged, and I knew I wanted to be the most godly husband and father I could possibly be. I also knew I had some areas of my life that needed sharpening. There was a man in my church in his sixties who was the most godly, humble, gentle man I knew. He was everything I envisioned a man of God should be. I wanted to be like him. I asked him if we could start hanging out together. He agreed. Over the next few years I spent part of every other week with him. His time helped shape who I am today.

What connects those stories to each other? The simple fact is we often are who we crave to be. We are whom we idolize. We are whom we hang out with on a regular basis. We are whom we position ourselves to be over time. The more I craved to be like my sixth-grade friends and the longer I hung out with them, the more I would become like them. Thankfully I had a teacher wise enough to recognize that fact. The more I craved to be like my adult mentor and the longer I hung out with him, the more I would become like him.

As followers of Christ, as leaders in the church, and as the church, we are to be people and be leading people, to be like Jesus. And, just as with my personal examples, the same is true in our walk with Christ. The more I crave to be like Jesus and the longer I am with Jesus, the more I will be like Jesus. In fact, that is essentially the very definition of discipleship...to be like Jesus.

A disciple is one who is becoming like the one doing the discipling. A disciple is a follower, but even greater than our thought of following someone, the biblical idea of disciple is one who is following in such a way as to replicate identically the person one is following. Jesus's disciples are not simply to follow Him geographically. We are to follow Him to be like Him in every way. Even more, Jesus told His disciples to make disciples. It is a continuous cycle of reproduction. That is the ultimate role of the church.

And here, perhaps, is the even greater issue. It's the one we know but may not readily admit. The more we look like Jesus, the more craveable we will be to a lost world who do not even have a personal relationship with Jesus. If we want to reach our communities for Christ, we have to become more craveable to our communities. Churches spend a lot of time and money making themselves attractive to their communities. *Craveable* reveals a secret that should have been obvious to all of us—craveable Christians make craveable churches.

If only there was a better way to understand, systematize, and explain the process to "go and make disciples" in a craveable way.

As a pastor, that is why I am most excited when a guy like Artie Davis comes along. I'll never forget sitting in Artie's office the first time he showed me the *Craveable* concept. My first thought was, "Why Artie?" Why couldn't I be the one to come up with this? Artie has simplified something all of us are trying to do and written it in terminology we can not only learn but also easily explain. Artie has captured God's mission in the world with amazing simplicity that everyone in the church can understand.

Artie's mission matrix in *Craveable* makes so much sense. No matter the location or size of your church—*Craveable* describes "what" God wants you and the people you lead to be. The "how" is the unique fingerprint of God on your church and your community. That is left for you to discover.

Craveable should be on the top of your reading list if you are feeling the urge to be more missional. The simple format makes each of the forty chapters so easy to follow and apply to life. No matter if you lead two or two thousand, Artie's book will have an impact.

The credibility behind *Craveable* to me is obvious. I know Artie Davis and Cornerstone Church in Orangeburg, SC—this is their awesome story; no, this is God's story! God has used a racially diverse group of craveable Christians to capture the attention of their community—for His glory! Read all about it. If God can do this in Orangeburg, He can do it where you live!

Don't overcomplicate God's assignment in your life. If you read *Craveable*, you will be see how to simplify your approach to church and fall in love with the people in your community—all for Jesus!

—Ron Edmondson
Pastor, Immanuel Baptist Church, Lexington, KY
Church planter and organizational leadership consultant

UNDERSTANDING CRAVEABLE

T HE TRUTH HURTS, but we really need to know how badly we are doing.

I want you to try something. Go to your computer and pull up Google and search "Why are Christians so...?" Google will give you the top searches that follow those words. At the time of this writing, the top searches were disappointing. "Why are Christians so...

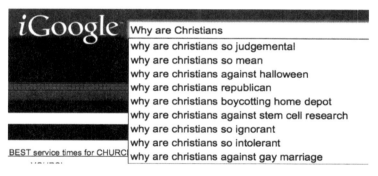

Do you see how people outside the church perceive us? Did you really believe it would be anything different? Look at those again. When you tell someone you are a Christian or Christ-follower, what do you think goes through their minds? For those outside the kingdom, probably something like, "Before me stands a judgmental, mean, ignorant, and intolerant person. Why should I listen to anything they have to say?"

I saw a bumper sticker that described the perception of Christians: "Lord, please save me from Your followers."

I can understand why most would feel that way. Sometimes I have prayed that same prayer! We are guilty! The local church and those of us who call ourselves Christians are primarily responsible for creating that perception. Jesus has called His bride to be beautiful and desirable! Well, how in the world are you supposed to do that when the people around you consider you "tolerable" at best and "detestable" at worst? That's right, detestable!

Church leaders spend millions of dollars each year on conferences, books, podcasts, and consultants. The mission is to make their churches more attractive and craveable for potential church shoppers. But the answers are nowhere near as complicated as we would all love to believe. The late Steve Jobs described a principle that applies as much in the kingdom as with Apple:

> Simple can be harder than complex: You have to work hard to get your thinking clean to make it simple. But it's worth it in the end, because once you get there, you can move mountains.[1]

The church will be more craveable to people in our communities when the Christ-followers in them become more craveable. Those truly reflecting the beauty of the kingdom of God should be "craveable" to others outside the kingdom, not detestable! Some may not agree with you or follow you as you follow Jesus, but the reflection of Jesus is not detestable!

People who watch you should crave the kingdom in you! A craveable kingdom is something that, once tasted, creates an intense desire in us to have more of it for ourselves.

> Craveable—a person, group, or gathering of people that so accurately reflects the Jesus in them that others greatly desire Him and to be more like Him

Have you ever thought of yourself as being craveable? Probably not, and most outside of the kingdom certainly don't think Christians are craveable—but we can change that. If you are a Christ-follower, you were designed, created, and empowered to be craveable! People should want to be with you. They should "crave" to be with you. It's all about how they perceive you.

You know we all have a "smell." Seriously. Haven't you heard people say, "She has this air about her." Yeah, that "air" is about the way people perceive us. We give off an odor. It's supposed to be an incredible, inviting aroma. Can you and your friends say this: "Everywhere we go, people breathe in the exquisite fragrance"?[2] Lift your arm and check yourself. We all need to. Go ahead, check yourself. See if what you are putting out is "exquisite" or repugnant. It matters, because everywhere we go, we are giving it out.

Have you ever been around someone who has spared no expense in their cologne budget? You can smell that as soon as they come in the room.

My mom always told me, "Artie, when you can smell your own badness, everybody else has been smelling your badness for a while." That's so true. We can think we're pleasant to be around, when actually we make people want to leave the room. We don't need them to run away from us; we need them to crave to be with us.

There is nothing like the smell of freshly baked bread. I can walk into a house with no appetite whatsoever, but the wonderful smell creates a hunger in me that drives me crazy until I get some. The only thing that can satisfy my hunger is a big hot slice, with real butter, grape jam (not jelly; it tears the fresh bread), and a big glass of cold milk. But I don't wake up in the morning looking for the hot, freshly baked bread and a cold glass of milk. That awesome smell wakes up a craving that I did not even know was there, and once it happens, I have to have some.

Paul painted a picture of a Roman military victory parade to believers in Corinth. These parades were common in Rome. They were similar to what happens in major cities in the United States after a professional sports team wins the World Series or Super Bowl. The lavish parades featured the hero of the military campaign: the general himself, along with his family and his soldiers. The "smell of victory" came from the priests who walked in front of the hero with censers emitting the smoke full of sweet incense. People associated the incense with victory.

Now, Paul said, you are that incense that points people to our victorious hero—Jesus Christ. So it is all about us (the aroma we carry) being all about Him (the way, the truth, and the life[3]).

Let's be honest; none of us has what it takes to have that kind of craveability on our own; we're just not that pretty and we don't smell that good! But we have what it takes within us to make that happen.

It's not us; it's Jesus in us. People will crave to be with us when we live it out.

A REFLECTION OF JESUS

We have to learn to "walk as Jesus walked." We need to do what Jesus did, talk as Jesus talked, and display what Jesus displayed. The "me" that I see in the mirror needs to reflect the Jesus I see when I read His Word. I need to:

+ Listen as He listened

+ Look as He looked

+ Love as He loved

+ Lead as He led

If we do that, people will stick to us like Gorilla Glue! Our craveability will be irresistible. I know you want to say, "I'm supposed to attract people to Jesus." That's true, but will they listen to you before they like you? No. If they don't like you, you can't expect them to like or crave the Jesus you're trying to introduce them to.

My daughter Leah is one of the most craveable people I know. When she enters a room, everyone's spirit is lifted. She has an incredible "air" about her that draws people to her like a magnet. She has been to many places and has had the privilege to meet with "kings" with which she has made positive impressions. She also has the ability to make a child smile, an old friend laugh, a new friend feel special, and to change the overall attitude when she enters a room. She makes a great impression, and she is genuine. In her short twenty-one years of life she has influenced hundreds of people, some who came to know Christ because they liked what they saw in her.

She has Muslim friends, agnostic friends, and a slew of other friends from various backgrounds and belief systems whom she truly loves regardless of their choices. She has gained such trust and influence in their lives by being a true, loving friend.

Understand this...

IT'S ALL ABOUT ME!

It's about the perception others have of me. Yeah, well, you too. Each of us has to understand and say to ourselves, "This is about me!" It's about me being like, acting like, and being craveable like Jesus. In this context saying it's about me is not a selfish statement at all! See, there's nothing craveable about me in my natural state. So being craveable like Jesus means "me" is dead! All people see is what He is working through me.

Jesus said, "I send you out as lambs among wolves."[4] Lambs are very craveable to wolves! Ha! I bet you never thought about that before! I don't think Jesus was saying, "I'm sending you out among those in the world to be torn apart by their big bites and powerful paws." No. He said, "I give you power and authority; there's no need to fear." I think He was saying, "Guys, just do what you have seen Me do, and people will find you so craveable. You will be like a lamb shank to a hungry carnivore."

I can remember what attracted me to the kingdom. In high school there was a girl who genuinely cared about me, and she did some simple but life-changing things:

+ She LISTENED to me.

+ She LOOKED out for me.

+ She LOVED me sincerely.

+ She LED me to Christ.

She made the first move to engage in a relationship with me. She initiated conversations, times together, and introduced me to her friends. She also invested in me. She gave me her time, energy, and even bought me cool stuff. Remember this: everyone is friends with those who give gifts.

During that time neither she nor any of her friends ever looked down on me, judged me, or left me out because I was not like her or her friends. They did just the opposite. They included me and made me feel accepted and loved.

When we put a true reflection of Jesus out front in our lives, where others can see Him through us rather than us in the flesh, it makes people run to us. "If I am lifted up...[I] will draw all peoples to myself."[5]

No matter how much we try to hide our heart, people will see what we do or don't do. Our hearts hold how we "feel" about people, society, political issues, and yes...God. So while others hear us, they believe God feels the same way about things as we do.

Jesus said, "If you have seen me, you have seen the Father."[6] Well, if we are to follow in the steps of Jesus, we should be able to say, "If you have seen me, you have seen Jesus." Not that we can be perfect or walk as the second person of the Godhead, but if people don't see the craveable Jesus in us, they will not crave the Jesus in us.

You know, the perception others have of us really does matter. What they think about us and what they see in us is how they will interpret who Jesus is. In other words, what they think about us will help form what they think about Jesus. So...

- ✦ If you act like a jerk, they will think Jesus is a jerk.
- ✦ If you act out in love, they will think Jesus is love.

How others perceive us, is how they are going to perceive Jesus. We are His ambassadors, and we are His representatives. Jesus said the kingdom of God lives in us. So what we do, say, and display will shape what others think about Jesus. They are then likely to carry that perception of Jesus they gained until they are exposed to another stronger, accurate reflection of Jesus.

If we think we know what is craveable to others, I can tell you one thing that is *not* craveable—our morality.

You heard me right. Your morality is not craveable! I hope you're not surprised at that statement. The truth is, people won't like you simply because you are moral. "What? You mean people don't want to have a relationship with Jesus because they see that I'm so godly?" No! They run from that! Do you seriously think the person who's out enjoying the life of self-indulgence looks at your life of self-denial and would say to you, "Your morality is so attractive. How can I be like you?" So don't get confused here about what is attractive to people.

This has been the problem in the church for centuries; we try to get people to follow us because we're so moral: "Don't you want to be like me?" See me. Let me just challenge you on this. If you think that your morality is going to bring someone into the kingdom, I can guarantee you it won't.

We can't run our morality up the flagpole of our "Christian camp" thinking that people will see. Then they will come running and beating the doors down, so they can be moral like us! What a joke!

For example, are you as moral as a devout Muslim? Muslims pray five times a day; they fast at least once a week. If their eye were to see pornography, it would be plucked out. If they were to steal, their hand would be cut off. If they were to fornicate or commit adultery, they would be stoned to death. They fast for thirty days during the times of Ramadan. Their first act of service each day must be of kindness to those they consider "the least of these."

Our morality is a by-product. Because we love God and wish to be like Jesus, we walk in His commands. "And does the master thank the servant for doing what he was told to do? Of course not."[7] So our morality is simply a product of our love, a by-product of our desire to please God.

Like Spam. You know Spam—that nasty mystery meat made of by-products left on the floor, scooped up, molded, surrounded by some translucent animal fat, and made to be fried and covered with grits! Don't wear your morality as some badge of honor; it's just not attractive. We must be moral, but it's not the thing we hang out as flypaper hoping some "lost fly" will be caught in our web of righteousness.

How many of you measure up to that? None! No one can compare to that. No Christian can be that moral. It can never be our morality that we think sets us apart and makes us craveable. Anyone from any religion can be moral. We have something so much bigger. We have Jesus coming through us.

If we don't become craveable to those around us, their view and concept of Jesus will not change, and consequently they won't change. We can't believe we've done all we can do if all we've done is flash our "kingdom card" and told others what they need to stop doing to get one. God has specific people we are supposed to touch, but then we have to be careful how and what we communicate to them. "You are you.[8] Now, isn't that pleasant?" Well, maybe not!

Every time we are in the company of or speak with someone out-side the kingdom, we must be careful. "Be wise in the way you act with people who are not believers, making the most of every oppor-tunity."[9] Every encounter is an opportunity for them to enter the kingdom by them seeing something craveable in us.

We have missed the standard. We look at ourselves as being righteous, moral, and the holders of great knowledge. But the very things we pride ourselves in are the things that are detestable to those God so desperately wants in His kingdom! Those outside should see God's kingdom reflected in us, and we aren't reflecting it very well!

We have focused on the standard of "holy" and not the standard Jesus set for what we are to be. Jesus was holy, so we are to be holy. But Jesus was craveable! And we have totally missed that part!

Being craveable is me being like He.

It's all about me!

Don't be offended at that statement. There is no pride in that. Quite the opposite. You see, "me" is you! We are the same. What I mean is we both need to take responsibility for ourselves. It's about "me" being like "He"! I have to do that; you have to do that!

We must change what people see and hear from kingdom people. We must reverse the slide to detestableness. Each of us, starting with me, must begin to step as Jesus stepped. Only as each "me" begins to walk as Jesus walked will this slide begin to turn. Then it will spread to others as they see the changed lives and communities powered by His church rising to the challenge.

It starts with me—me doing my part in the church. The church is composed of three interconnected parts:

1. Me (the individual)

2. We (the group)

3. Us (the local congregation)

But it is all begins with me!

We have to take responsibility for ourselves and for those around us—not just those in the church! God has called us to live and act in such a way that every person in every sphere of influence we have will be drawn to us. They should find us, well—craveable!

Being craveable is the only way to accomplish the mission each of us in the kingdom has been given. The mission will be repeated multiple times in *Craveable*. Why? Because I am passionate about the fact that we have overcomplicated church, and people are going to hell every day in our communities because of it. So read this and get used to seeing it.

At Cornerstone this is our mission statement, and our people hear it over and over: to help people find, follow, and be like Jesus.

This is what we must do. It's not a class or obligation we can opt out of!

This "backslide" I believe is correctable, but it must start in the heart. Say that with me, it must "start in the heart." That means not an institutional change or a denominational shift, but the individual Christ-follower who comes to grip with their "me," taking personal responsibility to fulfill what they were created empowered and destined to do: to "be fruitful and multiply." Again, it must start in the heart.

But what is the overarching mind-set? What kind of passion can fuel such a paradigm shift? A passion that reflects the true nature and heart of Jesus. A person who believes that the Christian life is a life of misery and pain is not that craveable. Some would say, "Jesus said we would suffer," and "What about those Christians in China dying for their faith? Now that's the kind of people we should be!"

Yes, you will suffer as a Christian. Just being alive in a fallen world will include suffering and persecution. You are swimming against a cultural current that is strongly against who you are. You're going to suffer. But God never intended for you to wear your "long-suffering" as a robe of "righteousness"! I don't remember the Bible saying Paul was singing "'woe is me" while suffering on a death march to Rome. Just the opposite, he was "rejoicing" and "singing praises." He was suffering, but he didn't have a sign around his neck that said, "Suffering Christian, in pain. Come join me."

Paul showed his Christlikeness by demonstrating his love for life and faith in his God. He was an example to those around him of a life that could rise above incredible odds and come out the victor!

Now that's craveable! And that's why others in the prisons with Paul also became followers of Jesus. Life was not working well for them. Getting out of prison would not change their lives, and I believe they knew it! They were longing for hope and a better approach to life. Paul's way was craveable to them even though he was in the same prison they were. Their circumstances might never change, but their view of what was going on could—and that was where the victory took place!

In spite of the high level of controversy and persecution that surrounded the first Christians in the Book of Acts, everybody did not hate them. The environment around them was positive and attractive to many, well, thousands! They were winners! Look how they were described in Acts:

> So continuing daily with one accord in the temple, and breaking bread from house to house, they ate their food with gladness and simplicity of heart, praising God and having favor with all the people. And the Lord added to the church daily those who were being saved.[10]

Favor describes how some people in the community felt toward this new movement that passionately followed Jesus Christ. The idea behind "finding favor" is described in the unusual craveability of the first Jerusalem Christians. People in the community did acts of kindness toward Christians because they were so nice! Could you imagine? This picture is hilarious. Can you see unbelievers meeting in the city square together on Saturday mornings to do random acts of kindness toward Christians? How about pagans having "Love a Christian" day at the local pagan temple? OK, maybe I am overstating to some level, but check it out; *favor* means what it says. It is something you do for someone.

People looked fondly upon the early Christians because of the life they lived and the value they brought to the community. They brought a new vibe of joy, peace, and kindness that embodied a different approach to life. They were craveable, and thousands came to the kingdom because of them.

That's what this book is all about. Imagine the influence of a single "me" who lives a craveable life. Then see that multiplied in "me, we, and us." They would be like the heroes God used to change people, communities, and nations in the past. Walking in the simple faith, power, and reflection of Jesus, they would capture the attention of people far from God. The Jesus the people saw in them and through them will make them craveable.

How to Use *Craveable*

Craveable is divided into nine sections with a total of forty chapters. Each chapter is meant to be read on its own, preferably one a day. These chapters should be read and then allowed to marinate with you for a period of time.

In each chapter you will see...

A target statement

This is the main thrust of each chapter. You can think of it as the "one thing" I hope you will take away from the reading. Look at the one point you just don't want to miss that makes reading one more book have the potential to be revolutionary.

A bullet point

The bullet point will inspire the action you need to take as a result of the target statement. Consider this the application point based on the target. My goal is for this all to be very practical. But I can't think for you, nor can I necessarily be the voice of God for you. And I have no idea of your context—city or rural, big or small, old church or new church...I don't know your community, your skill set, your role, or your culture. All these things make up your context, and only God can give you the "how" and action steps that make up the application. This book will be of value to you, and God will use it to change you if you choose. But that ball is bouncing in your court.

A burning question

Warning: the burning questions are tough! The burning questions are meant to burn. My heart is that God would burn His truth and Holy Spirit conviction about how you can become more craveable for Him. So the questions are there to start a deeper discussion u and God about next steps on your craveable journey. c they are meant to be used with your "we" (smaller group). ɔu overlook the burning questions, you will miss one of the c important parts of *Craveable*. So burn, Holy Spirit, burn! May od burn in "us" (His church) craveability beyond our imagination for the sake of the people in our world who have yet to meet Jesus!

PART 1

CRAVEABLE PERCEPTION

...to this you were called, because Christ also suffered for us, leaving us an example, that you should follow His steps.[1]

JESUS WAS THE most craveable person to ever walk the face of the earth. He drew huge crowds without Facebook, Twitter, a blog, or an iPhone with FaceTime! People would walk for days just to see and hear Him. The reason they did was because Jesus was off the charts with "craveability."

Jesus was pressed; He was surrounded by so many people that His disciples had to put Him in a boat. He fed thousands on a "remote" hillside—way out of the city. Thousands found Him, but think of how many others could have been looking for Him. Maybe there were thousands looking for Him but didn't know where He was!

When I say *craveable*, I use that word to describe the actions, words, and attitudes that Jesus displayed, and the thing that caused others by the thousands to be drawn to Him. It's the one word I think best describes how Jesus was perceived by those who had a chance to see Him and be with Him. It encompasses all the things He demonstrated, communicated, and imitated to attract them to the kingdom. You see, Jesus didn't just want to draw a crowd because He was on some ego trip. No, ultimately, it was about Jesus impacting the kingdom. That's why He did everything He did.

What people saw, heard, and experienced when they were with Jesus formed their perception of Him, and they found Him craveable. That's why...

1

PERCEPTION RULES

You will keep on seeing, but will not perceive...[1]

⬤ What people see, hear, and experience
with me matters to God.

WHEN I WAS in high school, I was the biggest turnoff to my friends. I began a relationship with Jesus when I was fifteen and was "indoctrinated" by some pretty religious folks. They told me that " rock 'n' roll is of the devil." I believed them and didn't listen to any of "the devil stuff." So one day I told my best friend, "God doesn't like rock 'n' roll." And he said, "Well, then, I don't like God." Wow. I blew that big-time. He made me feel like a heel.

We all have done or said things that have tarnished someone's impression of us.

HOW PEOPLE SEE ME IS HOW THEY WILL SEE JESUS

Perception describes the process whereby sensory stimulation is translated into organized experience.[2] In other words, people organize what they...

+ See—what they see us do and how we do it

+ Hear—what they hear us say or not say

+ Experience—what they experience through our attitudes and gestures

What people see, hear, and experience from our actions, words, and attitudes is their perception. That perception drives their attitudes toward our message and us.

It's all about what we...

- ◆ Do
- ◆ Say
- ◆ Display

WHAT WE DO

I'm so thankful that my high school best friend was able to see past my stupidity and eventually come to know Jesus. I had so misrepresented the heart and intention of Jesus that it may have had eternal consequences.

Have you ever watched the reality TV show *What Not to Wear?* It's about a person chosen by their friends for a makeover. The person thinks they look OK. They may even think they have style. They may say, "I like to look comfortable."

The problem is that they are not perceived as being comfortable. Others see them as a slob, an "I don't care" person, sloppy, and a mess. That's the most likely reason they ended up on the show and can't get a date.

The show plays out like an intervention. These fashion and style gurus first have the person wear what they think is appropriate attractive attire for work or a night out on the town. Then they put them in this tiny room surrounded by mirrors so the person can see themselves from every angle. The stylists ask the person, "What do you see?" Every single time the person is deceived! They may think they look one way, but they are perceived totally different! Then the style gurus train them, teach them, and literally force them out of what they feel is comfortable and into what is truly attractive.

However, there will always be those who will say, "I like myself, and that's all that matters." That is so untrue! We can't live our lives for us and ever hope to attract other people to us. When we are looking for a date, we don't try to look and sound our worst; we look and sound our best to attract the other person to us.

Many cultures, at one point or another, have believed our physical appearances to be a natural reflection of what kind of person we are spiritually. This notion, although casted off as ridiculous, makes me contemplate whether or not there is any validity to the theory. I cannot say that your hair color can tell me anything about you, but I can tell you that if you frown enough, my perception of you is going to be that you lack joy…and I may be correct. What you show to others often reflects what you have to offer to others.

There is a rule for those who are familiar with biblical interpretation studies in hermeneutics, and it's called "context is king." The rule is intended to give meat and truthful understanding to any biblical passage. By understanding what is happening, where it is happening, who is talking, and whom they are talking to makes much more sense out of the Bible. All these are so you see, hear, and perceive correctly what is being communicated.

Have you ever had to apologize for giving someone the wrong perception? I have! For example, running right by a person because you had to get to the bathroom. You are focused on one thing, and you see nothing but the bathroom door. Later you discover the person you didn't even see on the way to the bathroom thought you were a snob. No wonder. You walked (or ran) right past them and didn't speak. You weren't being a snob. You were trying not to soil your new jeans! But you were perceived as being a snob by the other person because of what they…

- Saw—you completely ignored them.
- Heard—you had nothing to say to them.
- Experienced—they felt ignored along with the wind from your speed as you passed them by.

Perception rules because it creates the context. If we create the wrong context, then everything else is seen, heard, and experienced in and through that context. So if you have the wrong context and the wrong perception, you get the wrong reaction.

Jesus was so good about creating the right perception. One example is seen in Mark's Gospel. A chronically ill woman sensed that if she touched Jesus's coat, she would be healed. Now, if I'm walking down the street and a random woman touches my coat, I may get upset. Jesus understood what perception was all about. In that moment He could have made the crowd feel loved or hated by how He reacted. But what they saw and heard from Jesus was His compassion and love. The crowd sensed the same thing as the sick woman. Jesus cared.

WHAT WE SAY

What we think of ourselves doesn't matter. Many of us have the "forget 'em" attitude. Most people think that it's up to them to try and be the best person they can. Their goal is to check all the good person boxes and miss all the bad person boxes. If they're doing that, then they're OK. That's just not true.

What others think about us does matter. We can't be all religious and think it's just about what we do. It's about what others see. What matters is how they perceive us. Don't misunderstand me. You may indeed be the greatest chef in the world, but if I watch you cook, smell your dish, taste your food, and think it's horrible, then my perception and experience tell me you're a bad chef! Consequently my perception drives my future decisions concerning your recipes, your restaurant, and what I tell others about you.

One of the most difficult things to do is look at ourselves objectively. So we have to depend on what others see, hear, and experience with us to understand the truth! I am not talking about the truth of who we really are, but the truth of who others believe us to be. What others believe us to be will greatly determine how much, if any, influence we gain in their lives.

The first perception others have of us could be called "first impressions." First impressions may indeed be an unfair type of human judgment because it can literally be based on a perception formed in seconds. However, any good career coach will tell you that within the first few minutes, or even seconds, you can secure or ruin a job opportunity. Why is it that people think they can make quick judgments about your character and be correct? Let's for now call it human instinct because we all, whether we say it or not, believe we have the ability to do it. And quite often we are right.

My mom told me, "Son, it's better to be thought of as a fool than to open your mouth and remove all doubt." It's incredible what comes out of our mouths sometimes, and when we speak, it's like toothpaste. Once you squeeze toothpaste out of the tube, there is no way to push it back in. Once words are out, they are just there. No retraction!

Even when we are wrong and have apologized for saying the wrong thing, expressing the wrong opinion, or insulting someone, it's difficult to wipe the slate clean.

WHAT WE DISPLAY

Many years ago a friend of mine was falsely accused of being a child molester. He was not a child molester. (I know because I was there when the accusation was made.) Others in the community heard these accusations, and, as you could imagine, with every retelling of the story it became more sensationalized and more widely exaggerated.

I would see people in social settings intentionally ignore him. If they were forced to speak to him, it was nauseatingly pretentious. You could see it in how they acted. Their body language, the rolling of the eyes, the turning of the head, and the faces of disgust were impossible to hide.

I live in a small southern town, and this handicapped him for years. He never really recovered. He had great potential and was a good friend, but the wrong perception of him destroyed so many things in his life.

Now, someone's perception of us doesn't change or lessen our value as a person, change God's love toward us or our "salvation status." However, our reflection of Jesus to others, the perception we help create, directly influences our impact on them.

And it's not just a one-time thing. The perception of Jesus by people closest to you is formed by their exposure to you over time. What we consistently do when things get hard, when we have a rough day, when our kids are giving us a hard time, when we find victory, when we realize our dreams have more influence than what we say, and our reactions to those experiences form others' perceptions of the Jesus we claim to follow.

Next, the perception we give others is the sum of what they see, hear, and experience with us—and what drives those is what we believe.

The perception of me is a reflection of Jesus.

What part of me is distorting my reflection of Christ?

2

WHAT YOU BELIEVE

"You are My witnesses," says the Lord, *"and My servant whom I have chosen, that you may know and believe Me, and understand that I am He. Before Me there was no God formed, nor shall there be after Me. I, even I, am the* Lord, *and besides Me there is no savior."*[1]

🔘 What I believe drives me.

Oh, wow! You're joking!" This was my father-in-law's response when I told him that I believed God wanted all men to become pastors. I believed that because that's what I was told at a young, impressionable age as a believer. I don't think I heard these guys right (I hope not), but because that was my understanding and belief at the mature age of twenty-one, it greatly influenced how I viewed God, myself, and other people.

I Need to Know the Truth—and Believe It

What do you believe? What do you believe about God, yourself, and other people? What we believe is foundational to everything else we do in life. It will all begin and be fueled by what we believe. So it's important to make sure that what we believe is the truth, the whole truth, and nothing but the truth. The only source of real truth is found in Scripture.

Now understand this. Just because something is true doesn't mean that it is true to someone else. I don't want you to dismiss that statement as some existential, New Age, humanistic nonsense.

Some of us in the church don't believe the truth about the truth. Some believe as long as they know the truth, as they believe it, it doesn't matter if someone else believes it or not.

No! It does matter. We must give people "permission" to not believe the truth. Many who were with Jesus didn't believe the truth right away. Just because we feel we have "told them the truth" and they reject it, we think we can move on. We couldn't be more wrong. That's not what made Jesus craveable—that's not what the craveable mind-set does.

A real kingdom-first mind-set doesn't seek to check evangelism off of a Sunday school checklist. It goes further than that. A real craveable mind-set is patient with people but also passionately anxious for them to know the real truth.

WHAT YOU BELIEVE ABOUT GOD

In this book my intention is not to change your theology, doctrine, or your denominational agreement. These issues have been addressed countless times and debated in many different forums. I don't intend to challenge any of your biblical understanding of real truth. My desire is to bring practical and challenging application. I hope to change a few paradigms and introduce you to a perspective maybe you haven't considered.

What we believe about God is the foundation and the core motivation of everything else that we do in life. So from the very beginning it is critical that we have the correct understanding, perception, and foundational beliefs about God.

What you truly believe about God will be the lens through which you see yourself, others, the world, and any opportunity that may present itself.

If I asked you to list what you really believe about God, what kind of list would you make?

+ God is always loving and giving.

+ He works *all* things out for my good.

+ He would never lead me to a harmful place.

+ He knows me by name.

- ◆ He has a great plan for my life.
- ◆ He can use me to do the supernatural.

Unfortunately all of our beliefs about God begin to be formed at an early age. Typically the dominant male in our childhood shaped the way we view God.

Psychologists understand this concept quite well. Fathers give their children their first impressions of what God is like. Kids who grow up in a home where the father is absent have real issues. They believe God will abandon them too. Children with perfectionist fathers grow up and, if they ever develop a relationship with God, have difficulty understanding grace and feel they can never "measure up" to what God wants them to be, causing them to carry a lot of guilt. Think back to your childhood. How has it shaped your view of your heavenly Father?

WHAT YOU BELIEVE ABOUT YOURSELF

As he [a man] thinks in his heart, so is he.[2]

Do you remember the conversation God had with Moses on the mountain at the burning bush? God had this great task for Moses, a huge task of rescuing over a million slaves and taking them to a new Promised Land God had prepared just for them.

In spite of the fact that the God of the universe was telling Moses he could do this (from a burning bush), he still didn't think he could do it. He wasn't questioning God's ability. His issue was that God couldn't do this great thing through "me." Moses was basically saying, "I'm the problem here, God, not you." You remember how people like to break up with others and tell, them, "It's not you; it's me." But they really mean, "Yeah, it's you!" Moses was giving God the old "it's not you; it's me" routine.

God was trying to tell Moses, "I know you're the problem. That is why you can't do it. I am going to do it through you. It's Me, Moses. My power, My glory. I just need you to believe I can do it through you!" Moses refused to believe that God could do it through him. He gave all kinds of excuses—until God got mad!

God saw Moses as he was going to be, doing things he was going to do as he walked in obedience to Him. Moses felt so inadequate, but God saw him as a superhero—the deliverer of millions, the destroyer of nations, the victor over invading armies, and the divider of seas! Yes, God did those things, but He wanted to do them through Moses. God works through people, if they are willing and allow the power of God to flow through them.

See, what we believe about ourselves is directly tied to what we believe about God! If we say we can't, what we are really saying is God can't. It's a fundamental flaw in our thinking. God can do whatever He desires, but He is always looking for someone to have the right heart and not believe in themselves but believe what God can do in and through anyone with a willing and believing heart.

> The LORD searches all the earth for people who have given themselves completely to him. He wants to make them strong.[3]

What we believe about ourselves encompasses our understanding of individual responsibility to God and others.

If you believe it doesn't matter what others think about you, and all that is required of you is to do the "right thing," you are handicapped in a major way—mostly because what we believe to be the "right thing" is just a set of actions that we have adopted through the actions or impression of other Christians, and it really has nothing to do with impacting others. It's all about making us feel we did what we had to do and the rest is up to God and the other person making the right choice.

We can't view others as the target for our righteous acts. If you see yourself as not having a lot of potential, then you will not have confidence to really believe in your potential to affect change in others. You will walk timidly and never initiate any move of God in the lives of others. How we view ourselves is huge!

It's all about me! It's all about you, and that certainly means a biblical and realistic view of what God has done, said, and believes about us.

WHAT YOU BELIEVE ABOUT OTHERS

Do you believe people can change? I mean hard-core change. When you see a toothless, homeless person who reeks of alcohol pushing a shopping cart down the street with hardly anything on, can you see a miracle there? Do you really believe in that kind of change? If so, are you willing to be used as the instrument by which God brings a supernatural, eternity-altering encounter through?

We must see every person as a miracle waiting to be unwrapped. Every broken, hurt, harmed, lame, lonely, and lifeless person is a potential launching pad for incredible change. If we don't believe that about others, we believe in a small God. And people pick up on that disbelief quite easily.

▚▙ I need to believe the truth about God, myself, and others.

❥ How can I get more of God's truth into my life?

3

WE DO WHAT WE BELIEVE

The beliefs we hold most deeply shape and deter-mine who we are and how we live.[1]

⬤ If I am not doing it, I don't believe it.

To really believe something means we are convinced of it. Generally we act on it without even thinking. It's a subconscious action out of complete confidence that what we believe is the truth and real.

MY BELIEFS ARE REVEALED THROUGH MY LIFE

Remember the Old Testament story about Isaac and his two sons, Esau and Jacob? Esau was the older brother and favored by his father, Isaac, over the younger brother, Jacob. When Isaac was about to die, he wanted to bless his older son, Esau. He told him to go hunting and cook some food for him, then bring it and he would bless him.

Well, the younger brother, Jacob, was favored by their mother, Rebekah. She overheard Isaac and Esau's conversation and devised a plan to disguise her favored son as Esau in order to receive his intended blessing.

Her plan of deception worked, and Isaac gave Jacob the blessing he was holding for Esau. The only reason he gave the blessing to Jacob was because he believed he was giving it to his favored son. He acted on what he believed to be the truth, even though he had been deceived.

How we act depends on what we believe. We all act in accordance

26

with our belief system. If we believe it is going to rain, we take an umbrella to work. Because we believe the weatherman when he says that it's going to rain, our actions align with what we believe.

Take the example of a background check. If all people spoke truth, providing us with a complete criminal record, why would we ever have to go behind their backs? If people would admit to every speeding ticket they've gotten going twenty-five plus over the speed limit, cops wouldn't have to walk back to their vehicles to run our history. Background checks are the basis of truth upon which an employer or a cop uses to determine their actions. So it is with our beliefs.

If we truly believe a biblical truth such as our need to help the poor, then we will have actions that demonstrate our compassion for the poor. On the other hand, if we believe something to be true that's not, such as interracial marriage is a sin, we still act on it and won't marry a person of another race; neither will we support someone else who chooses to marry a person of another race.

Whether our beliefs are biblically correct or not, our actions are driven by what we truly believe. Therefore many times, in order to change the way we affect others, we must first change what we believe.

Just like my belief in high school that rock 'n' roll music was sinful. I acted according to what I believed. However, when I understood that rock 'n' roll music was not a sin, I changed the way I acted toward other people who listen to that type of music. Changing what I believed to be true resulted in a small life change and a big reaction change toward others.

A pastor friend recently relayed a question to me that someone had posed to him: A son, who had chosen a homosexual lifestyle, asked his father if he could come home and bring his partner. Since the father had denied the son's request in the past, the father decided to call and ask his pastor what to do. This pastor had not decided what kind of advice he was going to give the father, so he asked my opinion. I told him that the father should let the son come home.

Jesus told the woman at the well to bring her "husband," although He knew her lifestyle choice was not that of a wife. He desired to see and speak to them both, knowing that His love would lead to conviction and a change of heart. I did not give my pastor friend specifics about sleeping arrangements or any other particulars; however, I am fully certain that the father will never have influence with his son if he does not show unconditional love.

There is a great chasm between the two worlds of acceptance and approval. It reminds me of the great chasm described by the rich man in the Gospel of Luke who was in hell and saw across a great space into heaven. If that father were to reject his son, he will lose the opportunity to have influence and speak into his son's way of life.

This father can hold to his convictions and in some warped way think that he has helped his son by demonstrating that his convictions are heavier and more important to him than his relationship with his own flesh and blood. What a travesty. What a waste. What a loss of opportunity for a father to help a son walk in the fullness of what God has intended for him.

I don't know the son's spiritual condition, but let's assume he is outside of the kingdom. Maybe he's considering his future, the spiritual place where he will rest his feet. Do you think he will consider, or seriously consider, putting his feet in the Christian kingdom if his father rejects him and holds fast to his beliefs? I seriously doubt that! Why would someone desire to become a part of something that makes them feel judged, condemned, ostracized, and unloved?

The perception of the son would not only be toward his father but also toward Christianity as a whole, and it would be that of contempt. His experience with his father will greatly influence his future actions, attitudes, and conversations about Christianity as a whole.

"Your heart represents the source of all your motivations—what you love to do and care about most."[2] As God changes my heart, He will change whom I love and what I do for them. So to become more craveable for Christ, everything starts with the heart.

I can't be responsible for anyone else but me. I must be intentional about changing the way other people perceive me. Remember, perception is all about what people see, hear, and experience when they come into contact with us. I must change, or attempt to change, what people experience when they have an opportunity to be with me.

Am I perceived as being craveable? I can't accurately reflect Jesus without being perceived as Jesus was perceived. That means I must imitate Jesus in what He did, said, and displayed at all costs.

Jesus cared what others thought about Him. He asked, "Who do people say that I am?" It mattered!

▥▶ If I am not craveable to others, I
need to change what I believe.

◊ Who can help me identify my false beliefs?

4

WE SAY WHAT WE FEEL

A fool vents all his feelings, but a wise man holds them back.[1]

⬤ My words reveal my heart.

ONE DAY MY wife, Georgie, and I were at the mall. We saw a couple from church we hadn't seen in a while. After the simple greetings I looked at the wife and said, "So when is the baby due?" After a small awkward silence, I quickly realized the mistake I had made. You guessed it; she wasn't pregnant. But she knew what was in my heart. It wasn't true and it wasn't pretty, but she heard what I was feeling!

My mouth will speak out of what fills my heart. Ouch! That hurts because there's a bunch of nasty stuff that goes out between these gums. Well, that's what Jesus said: "What you say flows from what is in your heart."[2] And sometimes I just need a heart change.

> Guard your heart above all else, for it determines the course of your life.[3]

Our hearts are like baskets that hold our emotions, desires, and hurts. The heart can be a very volatile place full of very powerful emotions that spill out in some manner onto all those we meet.

Have you ever had a fight with your spouse and then go to the grocery store still mad, trying to plan your great comeback attack strategy for your return home? Then you run into someone you know you need to be nice to and engage in a conversation with. Busted! You just can't do it. You try to get out of that situation as quickly as possible. The only thing in your heart right then is hurt, and you're thinking of revenge and a counterattack! No way can you appear craveable to that person. Why? Nothing good is going to come out of your mouth! You're too mad!

Our words are so powerful! In them is the power of life and death. When others hear what comes out of our mouths, it should bring life, hope, and power. Too often because we think lies instead of truths, our words bring death. We can kill the perception God really wants to reflect through us.

We were created in the image of God, and God created everything with His words. He spoke all things into existence. Now I'm not saying that our words are going to separate the sea from dry land, but just the fact that God creates by His words should let us know that there is power in the spoken words from the mouth of those created in His image.

Our words do create and destroy. I know I have felt devastated by the words that have been spoken to me by others—as well as been encouraged by words that have been spoken that gave great faith, endurance, and love.

WORDS AND PERCEPTION—AGAIN

Let me remind you of something: perception rules. We can think that what we believe or what we communicate to someone matters most. It's not. It's how you're perceived by others that makes the difference whether or not you're considered "a good person" or likable. It doesn't matter if you think you're likable if someone else looks at you and they don't like you at all.

Perception rules because the way that someone sees you will determine how they act toward you. You may think people will react to you in the manner in which you perceive yourself. Regardless of how we think, people are going to react not to what we believe of ourselves but to what they perceive of us.

It's just like the guy who has a large comb-over. You know that guy. He uses the comb-over technique to disguise his unwanted bald spot. He thinks the world is oblivious to his trick; he might even think he looks good. He believes he is hiding a flaw, and when he looks in the mirror, his perception of himself is skewed. What he finds attractive other people view in a different manner.

> If my heart reflects my words, then
> my words reflect Jesus.

What area in my life do I need to be more honest about?

5

WE DISPLAY WHAT WE WANT

*Even a child is known by his deeds, whether
what he does is pure and right.*[1]

⬤ How I communicate is as important
as what I communicate.

WHEN OUR OLDEST daughter, Rebecca, was young, she was strong-willed. After several seasons of discipline for her attitude, she found a way to show us she was doing what we asked. But she wasn't going to do it with joy! We called it the "slow blink." When we looked at her and asked if she had done what we said, she would look at us with a completely emotionless face and s-l-o-w-l-y blink her eyes. That was the only thing she could find to show her disapproval of our request. But her "slow blink" spoke volumes to us as parents. She was doing the right thing but in the wrong way!

Along with what we do and say, what we display forms someone's perception of us. What we display encompasses three things:

1. Attitude

2. Demeanor

3. Gestures or body language

We often call these combined characteristics the way someone "carries themselves."

What we display is our way of communicating what we want.

Nonverbal communication is huge. It carries much more weight than what we do or say. Our displayed communication can be intimidating, condemning, correcting, encouraging, approving, or loving.

OUR ATTITUDES

I can do and say all the "right" things and still not accurately reflect Jesus because I do those things with a bad attitude. It's just like Paul said, "God loves a cheerful giver."[2] The word for "cheerful" in the original language is where we get our word *hilarious*. The word describes a face that literally shines. Maybe it would describe your face while watching a funny movie or spending an evening laughing with family or friends. Maybe it describes your face when you watch your children in a school program. You can see it all over your face. Your attitude comes from your heart but ends up all over your face. And people know it—both the lost and saved people. Your face reveals what's in your heart.

It's not just about the gift, but rather it's the position of our hearts when we bring the gift that matters to God. I can be doing the right thing with a bad attitude and destroy the good I had just done.

It's like the Tower of Babel. God applauded their passion and plan, but they had the wrong purpose and the wrong attitude. They were doing something great, but the attitude destroyed all they had done.

I can also do the right thing while showing disdain through my body language.

We tried to teach our children the three components of true obedience:

1. Quickly

2. Completely

3. Cheerfully

All three of these components combine to make up our attitude. Don't do the right thing, even if it's obeying, the wrong way. Attitude matters!

Our Gestures

I remember one Saturday morning as a child when my dad took my cousin and me to get haircuts. This was one of those old-school barbershops, where you come in and sit in this long row of chairs and wait and talk to everyone else waiting their turn. Well, my cousin and I got tired of waiting, and we began a game in a vacant barber chair, which drew the attention of all the men waiting in the "chair row."

When I looked up, because of the deafening silence, all I could see was my dad's red face and his V-shaped snarled brow. I quickly ran to his side with the "please, O God, Dad, I didn't mean to do that" face. Rejected! I knew a heavy hand was going to greet me when I got home!

My dad and I never exchanged one word during that barber chair brawl, but we didn't have to. The display of attitude and gestures said more and communicated the severity of the soon-coming reprisal more than anything my dad could have said!

In his book *Enchantment* Guy Kawasaki gives four tips on what we can do to be more likable, or "enchanting," to use his word. Ultimately, we all want to be liked, and while personality plays a huge role, there are other things that can help. Here's what Guy says:[3]

1. *Make crow's-feet.* Smiling is extremely important when it comes to likability. Someone who is compared to Oscar the Grouch from Sesame Street is generally not an enchanting person. Smiling has to be authentic. People can instinctively pick up on a fake smile. A genuine smile engages not only the mouth but also the eyes. Kawasaki suggests thinking happy thoughts when you greet someone. This will cause your eyes to squint a little, making "crow's-feet."

2. *Dress for a tie.* Personal appearance makes or breaks a first impression, but to be truly likable, Kawasaki suggests dressing for a tie. Being underdressed gives the sign that you don't care much and/or that you are lazy, but overdressing can cause you to come off

as rich and above others. Dressing for a tie levels the playing field and instinctively disarms those in your company.

3. *Perfect your handshake.* Have you ever been handed the dead-fish shake when you first meet someone? Or how about the cold clammy hand? These never leave a good impression. Here are Kawasaki's tips on a great handshake:

+ Make eye contact throughout.

+ Utter an appropriate verbal greeting.

+ Make a "crow's-feet" smile.

+ Grip the person's hand and give it a firm squeeze.

+ Stand a moderate distance from the other person: not so close as to make him uncomfortable or so far away as to make him feel detached.

+ Make sure your hand is cool, dry, and smooth.

+ Hold the handshake for no longer that two to three seconds.

4. *Use right words.* Words are the vehicle in which we communicate. If you have a poor vehicle, you may not get to your destination. Kawasaki lists four tips on using the right words:

+ Use simple words. People do not want to carry a dictionary in order to have a conversation with you.

+ Use active words. Passive voice indicates a passive person.

+ Keep it short. Don't force people to listen. If they are interested in what you have to say, they will ask for more.

+ Use common, unambiguous analogies. Meet people on common ground. It is hard to stay interested in something you do not understand.

What we display to others in our attitudes, demeanor, and body language plays a major role in what others experience while with us.

▰▰ People have to like me before they will listen to me.

◊ Who can give me honest feedback about
how I come across to people?

6

BEING WITH US IS AN EXPERIENCE!

Keep a firm grasp on both your character and your teaching. Don't be diverted. Just keep at it. Both you and those who hear you will experience salvation.[1]

⬤ People's perceptions are more important than my intentions.

WHEN OUR THREE kids were all old enough and young enough to really enjoy a fun-filled vacation, we decided we would go to this incredible family destination spot for our once-in-a-lifetime experience. This spot was world renown, and we just knew we would be treated like kings.

We checked in to our hotel (owned and operated by the park), and we were in shock! It was dirty, stinky, old, and dingy. This place was well known for great customer service and creating world-class experiences. When I voiced my concerns, they were pretty much ignored.

Because our experience at this park was so disappointing, we left early and have never had a desire to go back. By the way, we found out, the hotel we stayed in was torn down two weeks after we left! Too bad they didn't tear it down before they lost customers for a lifetime.

> Experience—the totality of the cognitions given by percep-
> tion; all that is perceived, understood, and remembered.
> Or…Do + Say + Display = Perception

Whenever we have a bad experience, it brings strong emotions with it. Anger, disappointment, and frustration are a few of the more common responses—just as a great experience brings strong emotions like love, adoration, loyalty, and enthusiasm.

A vital part of God working through us to draw people to Himself is the emotions people have when they are with us. They see what we do, listen to what we say, and interpret our attitudes and body language. All of those things evoke an experience. And a major part of that experience is emotional.

Some people today want to downplay emotions. They want to take emotions out of the equation. They think "truth in" equals "truth out." If any emotions are allowed to play into the equation, the truth gets watered down, and being guided by emotions is dangerous. Part of this is true: we can't allow our emotions to rule over us and be the main source of guiding our actions, beliefs, or thoughts.

God made me an emotional person. The reason I am an emotional person is because God made me like Himself. Emotions give me joy, grief, compassion, anger, repentance, love, and peace. I can control these feelings to a degree, but that all comes with strong emotions. By giving myself permission to operate as an emotional being, I then accept the fact that I evoke strong emotions in others. So not allowing yourself to believe that emotions are a vital part of who you are will short-circuit the way God wired and created you to be.

When you're with someone and make a decision, there are almost always emotions and feelings tied to that decision. This may sound like a stretch for you, but we are partly responsible for other people's feelings. Listen, it's what happens in relationships, but probably most noticeably in marriage.

Let's say you do, say, or act a certain way, and your spouse gets his or her feelings hurt. Let me tell you, saying, "I'm sorry you feel that way, but that's not want I meant," helps nothing! It makes matters worse. Saying you are sorry that someone feels a certain way is like saying, "I'm sorry you are so stupid that you got the wrong perception of what I meant."

In a perfect world everyone would understand and perceive our "right intentions" and never become confused by our inability or shortcoming of communicating that intention. Most of us have good intentions, and we may try to tell and show others what we really mean, but many times it gets lost in translation. Our intentions are not what matters.

IT'S NOT INTENTION; IT'S PERCEPTION

When we hurt someone or disappoint someone, and it's a result of them not interpreting our intentions correctly, the temptation is to excuse the offense because that was not our intention, thereby putting the responsibility of the offense on the other person.

We have a duty to help create the correct emotional response to us. And that will never happen if we believe we can convince someone that the way they perceived our actions was wrong. It's not about our intention; it's all about their perception.

What I do, say, and display forms others' perception of me.

Remember, our "intention" matters very little. We generally have great intentions. We want to make a good impression, we want others to like and respect us, but all those good intentions are literally flushed down the drain by the force of others' perception of us.

I don't know about you, but I didn't ask my wife to marry me just because I liked everything I saw, heard, and accepted. No, I experienced powerful emotions when I was with her! Man, I was (and am!) lovesick over that woman. I never would have asked her to marry me without those strong emotions, without the experience I had when I was with her.

What we experience when we are with someone is the piece that completes our perception of that person and their message. When people were with Jesus, He stirred incredible emotions in them. You could see people crying, yelling, dancing, weeping, trembling, repenting, and being convicted.

Ever go to a restaurant and despise the experience? It could have just been that you had a menopausal waitress who turned the A/C up so high you were freezing and she was having a bad estrogen day, so she was short and rude. Well, the owner of the restaurant is in the back thinking everything is great. The food is good, it's coming out on time, and as he looks through the window from the back, most of the tables are filled; he thinks, "We're doing great." What he doesn't know is that menopausal Mary is out front freezing and offending all of his customers!

The owner sees several customers get up and leave mad. He runs them down and asks, "What's wrong? Was the food not good?" They tell him they never got far enough to taste the food. The service and attitude of the server was so bad, they left before the food came!

The customers leave, now believing that restaurant to be a terrible place. They never want to go back—and all because of menopausal Mary. The owner, however, has a totally different attitude and desire. Mary didn't reflect the owner's desires or convictions; she destroyed the perception of the restaurant because she forgot and didn't realize she was a reflection of the entire establishment.

Jesus told the Pharisees the same thing: "You guys aren't reflecting My Father's heart by adding all of these regulations to My people. You are destroying them by all of your rules. That is not the Father's heart at all!" It's so important that you and I don't act like menopausal Mary when it comes to portraying the heart of the Father. It's a big weight, but it's true. You and I can ruin other people's idea of the Father because of our actions.

My wife and I have owned a small commercial cleaning company for over twenty years. Several years ago a "manager" was supposed to be going around talking to our customers and asking them if the standard of service they were receiving was OK. Well, as the customers would point things out, he would become defensive and even lie about how things were done so as to lighten his workload in the coming nights.

We began to lose customers, and when we visited these accounts asking what happened, their response was, "Since this is the way your company treats its customers, we just had to go elsewhere." What? This guy cost us thousands of lost income because of his actions and attitudes with our customers.

The customers saw the manager's attitude as a reflection of our company's attitude. Nothing could have been further from the truth! But as a representative reflects the company, so then follows the customer's perception.

If I know others' perception of me is not as it should be, I can adjust my reflection. I have to change what I believe and how I feel in my heart, and what I display will change. These things will change someone's perception of me and therefore a perception of whom I represent.

We can't say, "I just have to do what is right regardless of how people take it." If we do that, we miss the heart of God. God's heart is always about showing His kingdom as attractive. I'm not talking about compromising the truth; we must reflect the truth. However, you can think you are standing on principles when you are standing in pride. And God opposes the proud!

So...if we are going to change the way we as Christians are perceived, and thereby greatly increase our influence and impact in the lives of others, we have to ask ourselves several pivotal questions:

+ Whom are we listening to?

+ What are we supposed to be doing?

+ Who should be helping us get it done?

+ Whom should our lives be touching?

+ What should our lives be displaying?

+ How are we supposed to do this stuff?

+ Where are we supposed do this?

I think the best place to begin is with the question: Whom are we listening to?

Truth communicated in love creates the best perception.

When do I need to care more about what people think?

PART 2
CRAVEABLE LISTENING

*A student is not above his teacher, but everyone
who is fully trained will be like his teacher.*[1]

WHAT JESUS DID was huge! He laid down a pattern and plan that would revolutionize the world. He was intentional in showing those around Him how to carry on the work He was going to do through them for thousands of years.

He planted the seeds of revolution in a rather small circle of untrained and uneducated men who were prepared by the Spirit to follow in the steps of this revolutionary. He trained these men to be attractive, irresistible, and craveable like Him.

We have to look at Jesus's life as a whole to capture His craveability. He was the whole package. We can't just look at one aspect of Jesus's life and expect to understand whom we are to imitate.

Jesus demonstrated to His followers how to be craveable, but it didn't begin with what He did in plain sight of others to see. Oh, no, Jesus's craveability began in a quiet still place, with His ear pressing in to hear the voice.

7

HE HEARD THE VOICE
OF THE FATHER

Jesus heard the voice of God, the Greatest Glory, when he received honor and glory from God the Father. The voice said, "This is my Son, whom I love, and I am very pleased with him." We heard that voice from heaven while we were with Jesus on the holy mountain.[1]

 Jesus needed direction from the Father.

A S A LITTLE boy, whenever someone would say something that was really great or hard to believe, I would say, "No way! You gotta be kidding!" And I remember my dad telling me one day, "Son, I have never lied to you, and I never will. I will always tell you the truth, no matter what." I never forgot that. It's vital to listen, but more so that whom you listen to is telling you the truth.

The first part of our foundation is establishing what we believe. Jesus set the standard of where we should get our belief system and its basis. Jesus believed what the Father told Him. He listened to Him to know what He knew would be the truth. Truth comes from the mouth of God.

When we hear God, we understand truth and we gain faith.

FAITH COMES BY HEARING, AND HEARING BY THE WORD OF GOD

I think one of the greatest spiritual disciplines Jesus displayed was His commitment to hear the voice of His Father. I don't understand why so many look at this discipline as some lost art that only Jesus and the early great leaders of the Christian faith had the ability or obligation to practice.

Hearing God's voice is not, as some have made it out to be, some "mystical practice" that belittles or lessens the power of the written Word (*logos*). Not at all! Hearing the voice of God was practiced by all great leaders and followers of God throughout Scripture, including Jesus.

Jesus said, "I only do what I see the Father doing, and I only say what the Father tells Me."[2] If Jesus heard from God this way, and we are commanded to walk as Jesus walked, and Jesus needed to hear from the Father to know what to do and what to say, don't you think we would need that even more?

If someone believes that hearing the voice outside of the written Word is not biblical, I would pose a simple question. How then are you to apply the written Word without hearing from God? For example, we are commanded to go and give the gospel to those who have not heard. So that command is in Scripture, and you want to obey it; then the question comes, "Where do I go? Whom do I speak to?"

If you don't listen to God for that answer, you will end up at the wrong place talking to the wrong people! Paul said, "I wanted to go, but the Spirit forbade me from going."[3] That was Paul carrying out God's command to go to the Gentiles. Then Paul had to hear where to start and who next; as he sought God, God spoke to him and gave him direction.

Jesus made it a regular practice to go away to a solitary place and pray.[4] Now understand Jesus was not just talking, He was listening. When Jesus was here on earth, He operated as 100 percent man. He didn't use anything or have anything that we can't use or we don't have! Everything that Jesus was, we can be.

> By myself I can do nothing...I seek not to please myself but him who sent me.[5]

> No longer do I call you servants, for a servant does not know what his master is doing; but I have called you friends, for all things that *I heard from My Father* I have made known to you.[6]

When my father told me that he'd never tell me a lie, it did something to me from that point forward. It made me that much more intent on hearing what he had to say. God won't tell you a lie. Jesus understood this. Jesus understood that hearing from His Father was vital to His mission. We have to understand that as well and listen intently and eagerly to His voice.

Jesus set an example for us to follow and set in place the model of what we must become and that we would do greater things than He did.[7] We could not be held to that if Jesus had something we don't have or don't have access to.

FOUND FAITH

"Without faith it is impossible to please God."[8] Well, if we don't have faith, we can't please God. I think starting with faith is a good place to begin. Apparently Jesus thought the same way. Since "faith comes by hearing, and hearing by the word of God,"[9] the place He found faith was listening to His Daddy.

Did Jesus need faith? Yes; without it He could not please the Father. He explained it to the disciples when they asked Him to increase their faith. They saw Jesus exercising faith and wanted to do what He was doing. Jesus said, "Nothing will be impossible to the one who has faith."[10] Well, naturally they saw Jesus doing things that seemed impossible, and if that was a key ingredient, they wanted more of it.

I think it's important to always remind ourselves that everything Jesus was, we can be. I'm not talking about "who" He was, His position as the second person of the Godhead, but what He was and what He did.

Jesus—operating completely as we are, all human—had to operate in faith. He couldn't operate in who He was; He had to operate in *what* He was—a man. Therefore He couldn't just command things to happen without the power of the Father working through Him. Well, He could have, but in doing so He would have destroyed His ability to command us to do all the things He did, because we lack the ability to do supernatural things in our own power.

I think that is what Jesus was referring to when Peter drew his sword to prevent the crowd from arresting Jesus. Jesus told him, "Or do you think that I cannot now pray to My Father, and He will provide Me with more than twelve legions of angels? How then could the Scriptures be fulfilled, that it must happen thus?"[11] Jesus would not operate outside the limitations of a mere man, nor would He step out of line with the will of the Father. And to do both of these, Jesus had to constantly hear from the Father.

FOUND COURAGE

After Jesus's baptism, "The Spirit came and rested on Him." This was His anointing, His call to begin His ministry here on earth. God said, "This is My beloved Son, in whom I am well pleased."[12] But before He could begin, He was driven into the wilderness to be "tempted by the devil."[13] Jesus's call, His ability to affect the future of mankind was about to be put to the test by His greatest enemy and hater, Satan himself.

The glory, the anointing, the authority of the kingdom, and all that God had planned for Jesus was going to be tested. I don't fully understand this principle of testing. It happened to so many from Job to Jesus to me, and Peter...

> Simon, Simon, Satan has asked to test all of you as a farmer sifts his wheat.[14]

This world is Satan's domain. It is his ground that was granted to him by God for a period of time. And this being his domain, he has the right to test any person God is using and empowering to take ground and damage his kingdom.

If we think we are going to be powerful enough, filled with God enough, have a calling great enough, and craveable enough to change the lives of those around us, understand this: the greater your potential to harm Satan's kingdom, the greater your testing will be!

I have heard many people say things like: "God has called me to pastor." "I'm going to plant a church." "I'm going to write a book." All those things are great, but many of those "callings" don't come to pass! The individuals wash out, they lose heart, they give up too soon, or they "sin out" and have to step down. All such callings will be tested, and we have to come out of the other side of the testing to "prove" the calling as real.

A scientist can say, "I have developed a human transporter. It will break apart all human matter and DNA, and they will be sent to a predetermined destination and reassembled in its entirety." Yeah, right! Just because you say that, I'm not standing in line to have all my "human matter" broken apart! Yeah, I gotta see some serious testing on that thing before buying a ticket! Just because you put a label on something doesn't mean it's legitimate. Nothing is real until it's tested!

▞▶ The Father directed Jesus to the right place at the right time, every time.

◊ Where does the Father want me now?

I HEAR THE VOICE
OF THE FATHER

Everyone who is of the truth hears My voice.[1]

 If I don't hear from God, I will never please Him.

PREACHED ON THIS once, and I said, "God has an opinion on almost everything concerning us." The next week a guy came by to see me. A little "distressed" about my sermon, he said, "God doesn't care if I drive a pink Cadillac!"

I asked him if he had kids.

"Yeah, three," he said.

"Do you have an opinion about where they go to school, whom they date or marry, where they go to college, or where they work?"

"Well, of course I do!"

"Why? Because you love them so much that you care about even the small things that concern them?"

"Yes, because I love them."

"So, what you are really saying is that you are a better father than God?"

"What? Of course that's not what I'm saying!"

Well, in essence that's what he was saying. Too often we don't understand how precious we are to our heavenly Father. He really does concern Himself about the smallest things concerning us. He is not too busy, uncaring, or "too big" to care about the things that are on our hearts. If we think anything less than that, it really is insulting to a loving Father who with all His heart is trying to demonstrate His love. If we say, "He really doesn't care about that," then God says, "You don't understand how much I love you."

I think it's impossible for me to fully obey the written Word of God without hearing God speaking to me personally. God cares about me, and He cares if I make the best decision. I can make good choices based on what I know in Scripture, the wisdom I have gained through the mistakes and victories I have had, and what I learned from others. And those choices would be "good." They wouldn't break any biblical commands or cultural rules. But hearing from the Father is the *only* way to make the God choice.

As a matter of fact, God promised His people coming out of bondage huge blessings "if you diligently heed *the voice* of the LORD your God."[2] As they journeyed along, they needed to hear from God at every turn. The Father even guided with a cloud by day and a pillar of fire at night. Both of those were outward signs of the voice of God. When the cloud moved, they moved. When the cloud stopped, they stopped. They understood, "If we don't follow God in the middle of this desert, we will be lost and vulnerable to our enemies." Following God was the only option!

God blessed those who listen for His voice and obeys it.

> And all these blessings shall come upon you and overtake you, because you obey the voice of the LORD your God.[3]

> I have obeyed the voice of the LORD my God, and have done according to all that You have commanded me.[4]

> Whether it is pleasing or displeasing, we will obey the voice of the LORD our God to whom we send you, that it may be well with us when we obey the voice of the LORD our God.[5]

> It is written in the prophets, "And they shall all be taught by God." Therefore everyone who has heard and learned from the Father comes to Me.[6]

> He who belongs to God hears what God says. The reason you do not hear is that you do not belong to God.[7]

God has an opinion about things such as these...

- Whom I marry
- What house I buy
- Where I work
- Where I go to church
- What school my kids attend
- Whom my kids marry
- Where I go to college
- What my major will be in college
- And so on...

I hope you get the point. None of these questions are answered in Scripture; however, we would all recognize the importance of making the "God choice" in all these decisions.

> He replied, "Blessed rather are those who hear the word of God and obey it."[8]

Some will say, "Well, I prayed about it, and I just *feel*...," or "I *think* God wants me to do this." You can call it what you will, but if you pray and ask God to guide you, you are asking God to speak to you! You may call it a "feeling" or an intellectual leaning that you have gained after praying through it, but the truth is you are asking God to reveal to you His desire for you in that matter. That is hearing the voice of God!

I LISTEN FOR FAITH

> If you have trouble hearing God speak, you are in trouble at the very heart of your Christian experience.[9]

Faith is absolutely vital to being craveable, because "without faith it is impossible to please God."[10] If we live and do life with others but don't operate in faith, we will not understand what we are doing from day to day and won't be reflecting the real Jesus. People won't find us craveable without faith. I know that sounds funny, but it's true!

God taught me a huge lesson on faith several years ago. We had added a third addition to our church building, we were holding multiple services, and we were once again out of room. Families coming in on Sunday mornings were leaving when they were not able to find seats together. Now watching that happen while you are preaching is like having someone pull your toenails out while you are trying to speak! Really, it's quite painful.

I kept telling God what the problem was: "We need to build a new building across the street on the ten acres we own." Well, I kept waiting for some sign from God letting me know it was OK for us to do that, but it never came. I was really tired of God not really doing what He was "supposed" to do in this situation.

One day I just knew that's what we had to do, even if God hadn't figured it out yet. I talked with our leaders and told them I really thought that's what God wanted us to do. They got on board, and I called the architect. He made some pretty little drawings of how this grand new place would look.

I presented this "new-practical-only-real-solution-to-the-problem" vision to the church, and they "dropped it like it was hot." No passion. No buy in. It just fell to the ground. I was so mad at God! My attitude went something like this: "Listen, I've done all I can do. If You want to let people continue to walk out of here every week when they want to stay and hear the gospel, carry on. But I'm sick of this." Or something like that.

I remember riding in my car and hearing God say, "Artie, you are going to have to learn what it means to hear My voice. If not, you will continue to make poor decisions." Well, that was the beginning of a yearlong journey of learning to listen to the voice of God.

I had to go to so many places just seeking quiet: rivers, oceans, forests, and a monastery! I couldn't listen to the radio, and it was physically hard for me to speak during that time. It was as if God just wanted me to learn to be at His feet and learn that He really does speak!

At the end of that difficult year I was driving down the road from my house and heard the voice of God very clearly say, "Artie, I want you guys to sell your building and renovate the old Winn-Dixie building up the street."

"What? Seriously, God? Our building is less than five years old. We have made three additions to it, and You want me to tell the church we are supposed to sell it and move 3.2 miles down the road and fix up that old abandoned grocery store? They didn't like the 'practical' idea of building across the street. If I tell them this, they will think I have lost my mind."

I knew I had to obey God, so I scheduled another set of meetings with leaders and eventually a Sunday morning when I was going to announce this new "God vision" to the church. I was scared to death. After I told everyone what we felt like God was telling us to do, the whole church broke out in thunderous applause. "No way! You mean you all aren't going to hang me for this? I mean, surely you all have to see how ridiculous this sounds." The bottom line is that when God speaks, there is unity, and unity commands a blessing.

We ran into some incredible external challenges getting that vision done! But the point I want to make is this: at every obstacle and mountain we were able to look at it and say, "Be uprooted and cast into the sea." Why? We had faith. Why did we have faith? "Faith comes by hearing, and hearing by the word of God."[11] God had spoken to me and to us as a church; this is what we were supposed to do. So we didn't doubt; we knew that we knew that we knew this was what God had said. Therefore we had the ability to push through any and all blockades. And it was done and finished just as He had planned.

See if you can follow the process God used to teach me the importance of faith:

"Faith comes by hearing, and hearing by the Word of God."

Not just reading, but hearing. Not just listening to, but hearing. "He who has an ear, let him hear."[12]

The first building I had decided was right didn't come by a word from God. It was my word. My word ain't gonna build faith. That idea was sin, and God can't bless sin. That's why it didn't work.

"Without faith it is impossible to please God."

So if faith comes by hearing and I don't hear God's voice, there is no way for me to please God! If we aren't hearing, we will make decisions based on our own understanding and not God's.

The upfitting of the grocery store—that can from God. We acted on this in faith. It was pleasing to God, because I heard it directly from His heart. God blessed the second building plan, and the people supported it because it was His idea. I had heard a word.

"Whatever is not of faith is sin."

This is killer for me. So I have to hear God's voice to gain faith. For without it I can't please God, because if what I'm doing is not based on faith, it is sin!

Really? This is a sin? I've been messed up over and over by this truth. That means I can do the "right" thing and still sin! I can make a decision that is "right" biblically but still be in sin. Listen carefully, and don't misunderstand what I'm saying.

> For God may speak in one way, or in another, yet man does not perceive it.[13]

I can buy a pink Cadillac, pay cash, have no debt, and it be a great deal, but if I didn't buy it hearing from God, I bought it in sin! Now, don't go crazy over this principle and start saying, "That can't be right! If that's right, then I have to ask God what color socks to put on. I don't want to sin by wearing brown socks when God wants me to wear black ones."

Part of hearing God's voice is walking in the Spirit. That means we are gently led in what things we need to do and not do. So if you're walking in the Spirit, you will just know which pair of socks to wear!

> When God spoke to Moses and others in the Old Testament, those events were encounters with God. An encounter with Jesus was an encounter with God for the disciples. In the same way an encounter with the Holy Spirit is an encounter with God for you.[14]

See, faith is so vital in dealing with other people in a way that is going to allow us to show them the real Jesus. Not everyone is the same. We can't have some predetermined presentation for everyone we meet in telling them about Jesus.

Only God knows the heart: "Man looks at the outward appearance, but the LORD looks at the heart."[15] Only God can see the real need in someone, so we need to ask Him. He knows what would make Himself craveable to that person or group. So if we listen, we gain faith, and we can then act and speak knowing, believing, and expecting that God will work in that person's life.

> The Spirit…will guide you into all truth; for He will not speak on His own authority, but whatever He hears He will speak.[16]

I LISTEN FOR ENDURANCE

> Dear brothers and sisters, when troubles come your way, consider it an opportunity for great joy. For you know that when your faith is tested, your endurance has a chance to grow. So let it grow, for when your *endurance is fully developed, you will be perfect* and complete, needing nothing.[17]

I can remember my wife and me having our faith tested several times in our lives. However, one stands above the rest. We both knew God was calling us to a great new chapter and season in our lives. As soon as this calling and anointing came, so did the testing! And it came with a vengeance!

We were in a state of faith testing for years. Those years were very difficult for us; the enemy came at us on every front with what seemed to be an unrelenting determination to destroy us. Temptations of many kinds presented themselves. (The enemy comes to kill, rob, and destroy.[18]) And we were tried, tested, and tired—tired of the fight. We wanted to give up and go our separate ways. The feeling of running away to a place where no one knows your name sounded like a good option. What a way to have blown things up! During this time of testing we came to understand the deepest meaning of what Paul said: "When you have done all you can do to stand, stand!"[19]

This is the deal. Satan doesn't want one single "me" to be like He (Jesus). The enemy of the kingdom of God loves for any believing "me" to fall down in defeat and stay down. He knows any person down and out isn't craveable! He or she can't attract people to Jesus, because a defeated down-and-out person isn't showing the real Jesus. Jesus isn't down and out; He is up and out!

Understand that when we set our hearts to be like Jesus, accurately reflecting Him and becoming craveable to those around us, we make a huge kingdom impact! Satan will not take that lying down; he will test you—just as he did Jesus, Job, and James. Since Satan is the "god" of this world, he has a right to try and stop any heavenly plan that would damage his domain.

> So you received the message with joy from the Holy Spirit in spite of the severe suffering it brought you. In this way, you imitated both us and the Lord.[20]

I say this to give you an FYI: the craveable journey comes with a price! Don't think that you can gain the understanding and tools necessary to really be used by God to bring great change to lives of others and go through without being burned or scarred. It will get hot, baby! You will be tested, and if you don't keep standing, you will be out of the count, out of the calling, and out of the game.

> We wanted very much to come to you, and I, Paul, tried again and again, but Satan prevented us.[21]

God has great plans and dreams for us. If we understand that and walk in it, we will be in awe of God! Is that something you do regularly, stand in awe of God? Are you in awe of how He has worked things out for your good in the midst of certain catastrophe? I hope you are, because God doesn't like it when we aren't in awe of Him.

> "Consider then and realize how evil and bitter it is for you when you forsake the LORD your God and have no awe of me," declares the Lord, the LORD Almighty.[22]

As Jesus was hearing His Father's voice and gaining great faith and courage for His journey, the time came for Him to begin His journey...

⟩ **Every day I need to know what only God knows.**

⟩ **What can I change to hear God more often?**

9

HE KNEW HIS MISSION

…you gave me a mission in the world.[1]

🔘 Jesus kept score.

I'M NOT A sports fanatic, but I do watch my son's football games and see the occasional game on TV. One of the great things about football is that it takes a team to accomplish anything. Each player at each position has a specific objective they want to accomplish each play. The linemen (my boy) block, the quarterback throws, and the receivers catch. That's their objective: to do their individual jobs. The mission: to help the entire team win the football game. The players' tasks may seem small, but the mission—that's worth getting dirty and getting tackled for.

There's a difference between a "task" and a "mission." A task is an assigned activity that doesn't have an assigned outcome, like a chore we would give one of our kids: "wash the dishes." But the mission might be: "Clean the kitchen in such a way that your mom won't have to do anything to it when she gets home." So that's not just a task but a series of tasks with the outcome being measurable and accountable (to mom).

To illustrate this further, let's take a military example. When a commander is given a "mission," it generally comes in two parts.

1. Objective: What you have to do—contains a set of tasks

2. Outcome: What you have to get done—is measurable and accountable

The mission given to the soldier might look like this:

1. Objective: "Advance on hill number 62 and engage all enemy presence."

2. Outcome: "Hill number 62 must be held by us until reinforcements arrive in twelve days."

In spiritual terms, mission is an assignment from God with two components:

1. A set of specific objectives

2. A set of measurable outcomes

If we take this understanding of mission and put it into everyday life, it generates two questions:

1. What must I *do*? (Objective)

2. What has to get *done*? (Outcome)

In Western culture we tend to be task-oriented people. We just want to know what we are supposed to do and then just let us go. Just give us the checklist (objectives) and tell us the "ministries" we're required to do. And after we have completed the checklist, we think we're done. No! There's another part. We are too quick to dismiss the outcome. We must own the outcome, not just complete the list of objectives.

Jesus said He did everything the Father asked Him. He completed His mission. He not only completed the tasks, but He also obtained the required outcome. When we know and become convinced of what we have to *do* and what must be *done*, it brings a weight.

There's a thing to know and a thing we must do that you know needs to get done. Pay attention to this thing that lives deep down in your gut. It's the thing I will call...

THE WEIGHT OF THE WHAT

That weight should not leave when we complete our list of objectives. If we continue to engage in the objectives (what we must do) and the required results are not achieved, we can't stop. The "weight of the what" must remain until we complete the mission. When the outcome is realized. When it is done.

Jesus understood His two "whats" very well.

"What must I do?"

Jesus's mission had three objectives:

1. *Give life to the lost.* "I have come that they may have life, and life...more abundantly."[2] He said, "I am...the life..."[3]

2. *Give the truth.* Jesus didn't just proclaim real truth; He said, "I am...the truth..."[4]

3. *Give the kingdom.* "You say rightly that I am a king. For this cause I was born, and for this cause I have come into the world, that I should bear witness to the truth."[5] "You have stayed with me through my struggles. Just as my Father has given me a kingdom, I also give you a kingdom."[6]

"What must I get done?"

There were four things Jesus needed to do:

1. Build and multiply followers

2. Establish His church

3. Empower His church

4. Unleash His church

Jesus's followers must move with Him until fully equipped and empowered to go out. His followers must reproduce themselves over and over from city to city.

> He gave his life to purchase freedom for everyone. This is the message God gave to the world at just the right time.[7]

If we look at the story Jesus told about the kingdom, where He likens it to the scattering of seed, I believe we will see that one of the points of the story is that we should be careful where we scatter our seed.

During Jesus's day no farmer would take valuable seed and scatter it on the path, rocks, or among the thorns! Any farmer would know the best and only place to put your seed is on the "good ground."

Now, since the ground in that story resides in the heart, and only God knows and sees the heart, who then should seek to ask where our investment should go?

If we were to put Jesus's mission on a matrix, and let's just call it a "Mission Matrix," this is how it may look.

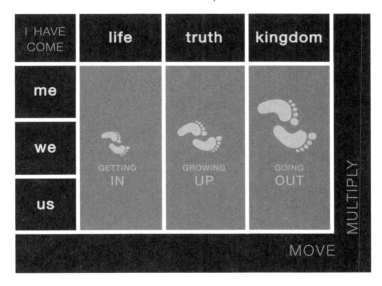

"I came to do what the Father told Me to do," Jesus said. He understood this "what I must do" very well. "I must do the will of Him who sent Me." He also understood what that meant: "to seek and save the lost." And He knew what must be done, which was giving His life to establish His church that would take His message to every corner of the world.

Can you see that understanding these two whats gave the framework for Jesus's mission? And Jesus's assignment—all He had to do, and all He had to get done—depended most on Him reflecting the essence of the Father, showing a lost and dying world the...

CRAVEABLE FATHER

Yes, God the Father is craveable! Jesus is an exact reflection of the Father. "He who has seen Me has seen the Father."[8] So when people saw all that Jesus did, said, and displayed, their perception of Jesus was how they saw the Father.

Jesus was changing the perception people had of the Father. The perception most had of God was displayed by the religious leaders of that time, and they were the ones, the only ones, whom Jesus was continually battling with!

So Jesus came along and did what the "religious" were not doing. He said what they were not saying, and He displayed attitudes they did not. Jesus knew most people had the wrong perception of God. So as He accurately reflected the Father, He began a movement to show the real heart and character of God.

⫸ Jesus won through multiplied followers.

🔥 How can I take my investment in Christ-followers to another level?

10

I KNOW MY MISSION

I want to carry out the mission *I received from the Lord Jesus—* the *mission of testifying to the Good News of God's kindness.*[1]

🔘 My life is my mission.

I LOVE THE STORY of "Jack and the Beanstalk." I guess it's because I have always been one who is looking for the magic. Just doing something so I can pay the bills and survive is so boring and mundane! I like the magic bean approach. I like giving my life and energy to something that's not just going to turn out to look normal and average.

THERE IS NO PLAN B; IT'S JUST YOU AND ME!

I think living a life that is full and God pleasing was designed by God to be simple. We have overcomplicated something that every believer should be able to successfully follow. That means since the time of Jesus to now, every nation and village, every child and senior, every illiterate and graduate should understand what is required of them by God in the simplest form. Then they should be able to understand it well enough to share it and teach it to someone else. That is kingdom growth.

> But I fear, lest somehow, as the serpent deceived Eve by his craftiness, so your minds may be corrupted from the simplicity that is in Christ.[2]

The craveable church was designed by God to be a simple thing. Unfortunately we have taken that simple process and morphed it

63

into something that is complicated and cumbersome. The process of becoming craveable to others is something that should be simple enough to teach a third-grader. If it is not simple enough to be taught by a sixth-grader, then many people become excluded whom God intended to be productive parts of the kingdom. People get left out because they can't teach someone to do what they need to do. It has been presented as so complicated, someone would feel inadequate trying to reproduce it.

Do this: take a modern translation of Scripture and flip through the Gospels of the New Testament; then just look at the section summaries—you know, those little one-line descriptions giving a summary of what you are about to read. If you do that, you will notice what Jesus did to carry out His mission.

Jesus's public ministry as summarized in the four Gospels can be divided into four activities:

1. Teaching His followers—39 percent

2. Performing miracles—23 percent

3. Preaching to crowds—20 percent

4. Rebuking the religious—18 percent

If that is how Jesus divided His time (a summary of activities, not an accurate accounting of every act and with whom), and if we are to walk as He walked and then imitate Him and do greater things than He did, I would think we must have some element of all the activities of Jesus present in our lives. We can't say we are going to be like Jesus and not do what Jesus did. That's ludicrous!

We can't accurately reflect a craveable Jesus to a lost and lonely world, without doing, saying, and displaying the things Jesus did. Anything less will not project to others nor give them the real Jesus perception in us.

"As the Father has sent Me, I also send you."[3] In other words, "It's Me and you, baby! Me and you!" That's still true. It's me and you! Me first. Yes, I have (you have) a mission. God the Father gave Jesus His mission. And now Jesus has given us a mission, not unlike His own. Our mission is very similar to that of Jesus's. As a matter of fact, it's like part B.

THE WEIGHT OF THE WHAT

Objectives: "What I must do?"

1. Help people find, follow, and be like Jesus

2. Be the church of me, we, and us

Outcomes: "What I must get done?"

1. *Make* followers of Jesus

2. *Move* myself and others

3. *Multiply* myself and others

I need you to read that again. Our first objective as Christ-followers is to help people find, follow and be like Jesus.

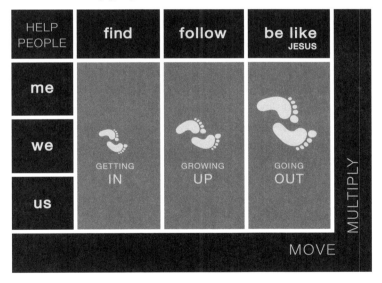

Mission is the "what" and incarnation is the "how."[4]

That is nonnegotiable. We can't opt out of it or drop out of it. That's what we're appointed and anointed to do. Write it down. I want you to marinate on this for a minute. Scripture says that when you come into a relationship with Jesus Christ, "you are not your own . . . you have been bought with a price."[5]

Our life's mission should be big enough that it touches every part of our lives. At no time does our mission ever stop, and at no time do we take a day off. How we approach our mission will change over time as our circumstances change, but our mission keeps burning hotter in us as we walk in it.

We can't accept salvation without accepting the mission that comes with it. Some want to accept Jesus and then show up at heaven's gate, flash their "kingdom card," and say, "I'm a member. I haven't done anything for the kingdom, but I plan to enjoy its benefits for a long time." Oh, no.

Jesus said, "If you love Me, you will keep My commands."[6] So if we love Jesus—and we have to love Him to be in the kingdom—we will keep His commands. His last command was to give us our mission. We have to be engaged in the mission. If we don't, then we have to just keep it real and say, "I just don't love Jesus enough to do what He said."

> They are not of the world, just as I am not of the world....As You sent Me into the world, I also have sent them into the world.[7]

God has called us to impact the lost and lonely, and we're not going to find them on the field. They're going to be off the field. When you look the Father in the eyes, He's not going to ask if you did everything right; He's going to ask whom you helped find, follow, and be like Jesus.

WHAT I MUST DO?

- ✦ Help people. I can't do this if I'm not involved with people. I know that sounds quite obvious, but many overlook the obvious. We need a crowd of people we are trying to impact on a regular basis. Oh, yeah, I must do that.

- ✦ Help people find Jesus. I can't if there are no people around me that I've heard God call their names. When I say "call their names," I mean we are listening and walking in step with the Spirit, and the Spirit speaks and draws us to certain people. They are your and my assignment.

- Help people follow Jesus. I can't if there are no
  people for me to teach. Once someone finds Jesus,
  they must learn to follow Jesus. And following Jesus
  can't just be taught; it must be caught. It's something
  that takes close contact. We have to be with them.
  It takes time. We have to get up in people's business
  and let them up in ours. We have to be patient and
  invest in them. They have to have time to "catch it."

- Help people be like Jesus. I can't if people aren't
  watching me be like Jesus. Again, this is no class-
  room. This is day-to-day, check-to-check life. Just as
  Jesus did it—eating, grilling, crying, laughing, and
  loving together.

What Must Be Done

Make: I have to make followers of Jesus.

"How can I make someone follow Jesus?" Well, you can't. But we
are commanded to do that very thing. So how does that work? "No
one can come to Me unless the Father who sent Me draws him."[8]
This is it. The Father and the Spirit draw people through me! It's all
about me! Well, not me, but "me" being willing to listen and be used
by God to draw people to Jesus.

If I'm surrendered to God's purpose and the Spirit's prompting,
then I will make followers of Jesus. My ability to obey the command
of God directly depends on my listening and surrendering to God.

So, if I'm not making followers and if I'm not bringing others
into the kingdom, then there's only one explanation for that: I'm
not listening and surrendering to God. God gives us the surety of
His Word to carry out and complete our mission. It is all through
His power.

Move: I must live a life where I move in two directions.

1. *More devoted to God:* Looking at our "mission
   matrix," moving from just "getting in" to being like
   Jesus is a move of devotion. That move takes a lifetime. Then as I become more devoted, I have to take

others with me. I take responsibility and become "my brothers' keeper" and help them become more devoted to God.

2. *More engaged with others:* It all starts with me, but it's all about me doing life with my "we" (smaller group) and "us" (the church). So the more engaged with others I become, the more effective I will be. I become engaged with other believers to help them and allow them to help me.

I also become more engaged with those on the outside. The more I'm involved with them, the more of an impact I will have.

I also take others with me to becoming more engaged. I help others see their need for their own "we" and "us." I get others excited about engaging with those outside, encouraging them to make intentional relationships and contacts.

Multiply.

One of the greatest joys in life is having babies! Seeing another human being find their place in the kingdom of God as a direct result of your investment and love is life changing. But an even greater joy than that can be had: having a grandchild. I have heard so many people say, "If I could have had my grandkids first, I would have."

These are the results God is holding me responsible for. This is the finish line, the outgoing mailbox, the checked box, the signed, sealed, and delivered product. We want to hear "Well done" from the Father. We want to say, as Jesus did, "It is finished."

WHILE I'M GOING

God's mission for me is not a destination but a lifestyle. This is just doing life! As you go, while you go, or on your way, keep the goal in mind.

Have you ever been to the beach and gotten caught in an undertow? An undertow is a current of water under the surface that you can't really see. But when standing still, you can feel the pull at your feet! It's hard to stand still in an undertow.

Our mission is like an undertow; it's the current that keeps us on track, moving in the flow of the kingdom and the Spirit. I've been at the beach many times watching my kids play in the water. They would enter the water at one place—playing, laughing, and jumping. Then before you realize it, they are way down the beach! They were moving and didn't even realize it!

That should be our life. There is a big difference between these two statements:

1. This is my mission in life.

2. This is my life in mission.

The first view separates life and mission. For instance, I have to do life and then I make my mission in life a priority when I can or when I have time to "work in it."

The second view sees life and mission as two inseparable components of the same journey. Mission and life in mission are two lines that are never seen. They melt together and look like a candy cane, beautifully bound together.

This is just how we live. We do life in mission. It gives meaning and purpose to everything we do. If I ever lose sight of why I'm doing something, it's so easy to get caught up in the "things" of life and feel like nothing really matters. But it all matters—everything matters in the kingdom.

If my life is my mission, then my
mission is worth measuring.

What is worth measuring in my mission for God?

PART 3

CRAVEABLE LOOKING

*The eyes of the LORD search the whole earth in order to
strengthen those whose hearts are fully committed to him.*[1]

TOLD MY MAMA as a little boy, "Mama, I'm going snake hunting."
She told me, "Son, be careful what you look for; you may end
up finding it." I have passed the same advice on to my children
on more than one occasion. All of us look for something, and that
"something" is not always the right thing.

We need other people for our journey. In fact, we more than need
them; they are necessary for us to get everything done that God
wants. But we need to make sure we are looking for the right people.
Just anybody is not good enough.

God is already at work in the lives of people you meet every day.
Your best time and energy must go toward the people in whom God
is already working. God loves everybody, but He has chosen some
just for you.

You are not just looking to make "converts" or "followers," but
you are also making disciples, who will continue to make disciples,
who will continue to make disciples. And your mission is not to win
one or a few to Jesus; neither is your goal simply to work hard for
Jesus. Your goal is to see hundreds, thousands, and even millions
find life in Jesus. In other words, "results" are the target, not good
intentions—God's results.

Am I making you nervous? Does it sound like I am saying you
should pour into the best, the brightest, or the richest people in
your life? Am I am telling you that you need to think like an NFL
scout? The average team in the National Football League spends

approximately $2 to $3 million a year trying to find new players!
And my source said that is not enough![2] What? The scout wants to
know:

1. Who runs the fastest?

2. Who jumps the highest?

3. Who is the strongest?

4. Who will make our team look good?

5. Who will help our team win?

Culture may tell you to do it that way, but God tells you the
opposite. One example is David, the shepherd boy who became
king. David's story involves an old prophet named Samuel. God was
fed up with the King Saul's behavior, so he told Samuel to go find
another king. And God told Samuel that the new king was one of
Jesse's sons.

To make a long story short, Samuel invited Jesse and his sons to
meet with him. Jesse's oldest and strongest son, Eliab, was the first
son that Samuel saw. He knew Eliab had to be the one God wanted
as king, but God said no. God told him that He looked past the first
impressions all the way to the heart and that Eliab was not the guy.

Although Jesse's seven older sons seemed to be a better choice,
God choose David, the youngest. In fact, David was so insignificant
that his daddy did not even invite him to the meeting with Samuel.
So God-choices are not obvious to the naked eye. But give Samuel
credit; because he was looking and listening to God, he did make
the right choice.[3]

So God has choices for whom you are to invest your life in.
Those choices will not always make sense, but remember that God
is looking at the heart. How do you find those people with whom
God is already working? Now get ready for this answer—you will
be impressed with my brilliance—ask Him! I know no other way to
find out unless God tells you. See the example of Samuel and David
again.

So let me review:

1. God is already at work in the lives of people in my world.

2. God wants me to invest my time and energy where He is already working.

3. I find out who those people are by asking God.

4. In obedience to God, I will find those people and invest my all in them.

Why is this most basic truth from God so important? I've been in contact with hundreds of leaders and churches. Most of them all work amazingly hard for God. But few of them are getting the results I know God wants. All of us must learn to work like Jesus and with Jesus, which includes looking for people with whom God is already at work. The goal is kingdom results, not hard work and good intentions.

11

HIS "ME" BECAME GOD'S "ME"

*Though he was God's Son, he learned trusting-
obedience by what he suffered, just as we do.[1]*

 Jesus struggled with obedience.

I WANT A BLACK worship leader" was my cry before the Lord as
we were searching for our first full-time worship leader at Cornerstone. We are a multiethnic church, and I really wanted an
African American guy on stage leading music, really bad!

As I continued to pray for that very thing, it became obvious that
was not God's plan. As a matter of fact, when God revealed to me
who it needed to be, I just didn't agree! I was like, "God, come on.
That can't be right. What about this, and this, and yeah, that other
thing too?" I had in my mind what I wanted so badly, and I was
having a hard time surrendering to God. But it turns out His choice
was the best choice. Go figure.

We all have difficulty laying down our own wants and desires. It's
hard to accept or say, "OK, maybe what I want isn't the best." To be
genuinely open, to embrace God's choices does not come natural to
me. Even Jesus had a hard time with that.

One of the first objectives in Jesus's mission was to ensure the
continued growth of the kingdom. That would mean finding the
right people to invest in to ensure that would take place. But He
first had to discover the fullness of His destiny and fully embrace
His mission in the world. Basically He had to find Himself—who
He was really meant to be. He had to find His "Me."

Jesus had to choose to follow the Father's plan for His life. He said, "By myself I can do nothing...I seek not to please myself but him who sent me."[2] Jesus had to choose between His "Me" and God's "Me." He said He didn't seek to please Himself. If He had, it would have been different from what the Father wanted for Him.

His "Me"

Jesus was fully human. He was 100 percent the same "stuff" we are. Jesus felt the things that humans feel and struggled through the same things we struggle through. Even though He was God's Son, His humanity still caused an intense struggle with His "Me." God's Word confirms Jesus's struggles: "For we do not have a high priest who is unable to sympathize with our weaknesses, but...one who has been tempted in every way, just as we are—yet was without sin."[3]

Remember that as Jesus struggled with His appointment with a brutal death on the eve of His betrayal, He cried out, "Father, if it's possible, let this cup of suffering be taken away from me. But let your will be done rather than mine."[4] In the flesh, Jesus didn't want to go to the cross. He endured the cross, and He despised the shame it brought to Him.

We forget that Jesus felt pain the way we do, understood temptation, and was drawn to satisfy the flesh and not the spirit. He had a "Me" inside of Him that had to die so His God "Me" could walk in full obedience to the Father.

His God "Me"

He emptied himself...[5]

The only way for Jesus, in human form, to become all the Father wanted Him to be was to have none of Himself left and be emptied out. Your God "me" is the person God intended for you to be. God told His frustrated followers in the Old Testament, "'For I know the plans I have for you,' says the LORD. 'They are plans for good and not for disaster, to give you a future and a hope.'"[6] He assured His people, in spite of their disappointment, that He had something big planned for them. He had a God "me" that was far better than anything their "me" wanted.

The Spirit was referred to as "water" in the Bible.[7] That reminds me of how my momma taught me to get all the ketchup out of the bottle. First, squeeze out all the ketchup. Next, put some water in the bottle and shake it up. The water cleared all the ketchup off the sides and the neck of the bottle. Then you could take the cap off and pour the remnant out. The bottle would be completely clean, all poured out and emptied of all the ketchup. If you didn't do that, anything else you put in that bottle would be contaminated by the ketchup left on the sides of the bottle.

If we leave any of our "me" in us, it will certainly contaminate the voice and will of God for us! Things get cloudy. The Spirit is clean, fresh, and powerful. God wants all of us with nothing left behind, if we are to operate at full capacity.

That's what Jesus did; He was completely emptied of all remnants of self.

I see the biggest issue for finding the "me" God intended us to be was what Jesus displayed when He prayed in the garden—surrender.

True surrender was seen when Jesus prayed, "Yet I want your will to be done, not mine."[8] "Not My desire, God. You know My heart. You know what I want, but that will never be the best. Give Me what You want. Make Me who You want to make Me."

His great mission went far beyond what He could get done in a mere three and a half years (He was all man). The Father and Jesus had a plan to ensure that "this gospel of the kingdom will be preached in all the world."[9] The Father's plan for reaching the nations today requires us to be like the ketchup bottle, emptied of our will. To find our "God me" is to find the person whom God needs and calls us to be.

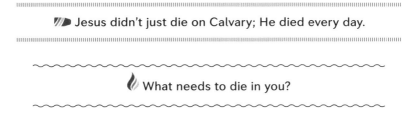

Jesus didn't just die on Calvary; He died every day.

What needs to die in you?

12

MY "ME" BECOMES GOD'S "ME"

*You are Christ's body—that's who you are! You must
never forget this. Only as you accept your part of
that body does your "part" mean anything.*[1]

⬤ Only when I die to self will I
become the "me" God intended.

ELF MUST NOT only be dead, but buried out of sight, for the
stench of the unburied self-life will frighten souls away from
Jesus."[2]

I remember being in my early twenties and standing in front of
the mirror, looking at every little detail of my face—every color, spot,
hair, and pimple. Then I said aloud, "Who are you, Artie Davis?" I
was struggling with my future, my upcoming marriage, what my life
was going to be, and who I was going to become.

I would imagine most of us have asked ourselves that question in
one form or another. We all want to know that what we are doing,
who we are, and where we are going is best.

The church starts with me.

Remember, it's all about me (and you). I am the church, and I
must be in the purpose of God with both feet. Watching from the
corner of the field like a fan or a coach is not enough. I must be in
the game. Most of us have never thought of ourselves as being the
church. We generally think the church is a building housing a group
of people under a sign designating what they believe.

But the church of Jesus Christ is so much more. It's you and me!

We are the church. I am the church, and everywhere I go, I take the church with me. And watch this: because Christ is in me, I take *Him* everywhere I go. Just as Mary was before the baby Jesus was born, we should walk around "pregnant with Jesus." We should be able to say, "My soul magnifies the Lord."[3] Can you imagine the glow on her face? There was life inside of her. That life was the Son of God Himself. How craveable was that? That same life is in me. Whoever sees me should see a reflection of the bride of Christ.

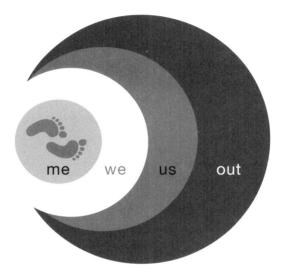

THE CHURCH IN ME

The church in "me" is only as powerful as I am surrendered to the Spirit of God.

Jesus said, "The kingdom of God is within you."[4] The power and ability I have to carry out the mission of the kingdom is generated by the kingdom in me being worked out.

Ever know someone who had a great treasure and buried it? It reminds me of the parable of the talents. The story is about three servants. The first servant was given five talents (money), the second was given two talents, and the third was given one talent. The first two handled what was given them well by investing their talents. The last one buried his talent (the kingdom).

When the master returned, he praised the first two, but the

last one he called wicked and threw him outside among the lost to suffer![5] God takes seriously what He has given us. He has not given us all the same amount, but He expects us to use what we have for Him. Fear cannot stop us from investing His life in others; neither can shame. We must invest what He has given us in the right places and watch Him give the return.

That's the kingdom in us and in me! The kingdom is in me, and I'm required to show the kingdom to others in a way that will cause others to be attracted to me so that the kingdom is multiplied.

When Jesus sent out the seventy followers to do the things He had been doing, He told them to go to the city. When they were invited into a house, they were told to stay, to bless the house, and to receive provision from the people. But they were instructed that if they were rejected in a city to go outside the city gates and shake the dirt from their shoes. Then they were to say, "The kingdom of God has come near you,"[6] meaning, "The kingdom came really close, but you missed it."

Interesting that the message the seventy were told to give was essentially the same no matter the response. Both those who accepted them and those who did not were to hear the message of God's kingdom. But the group who accepted the messengers (and their message) would experience the kingdom on the inside of them (much better). Those who rejected the message would experience the kingdom outside of them (not good).

This issue is weighty. You can be close to the kingdom on your spiritual journey but not "there." And you are not there until you are there. As I have always heard, close only counts in horseshoes and hand grenades. I fear that many who sit in American churches are close but not yet there. The implications are scary.

The one who doesn't receive, the kingdom only comes near. But if they receive the kingdom, it becomes personal and precious to them. They, in essence, own the kingdom (in a good way).

The church is in me, the kingdom is in me, and Jesus is in me. I now have the power not only to bring the kingdom near someone but also to help make the kingdom personal and precious to them. I want to give them something that becomes theirs that they can own. The kingdom is delivered through the power to change. That is what Jesus told His followers to do, and that is what we are called to do! Listen to God, listen to others, look for the opportunities, and release the power of God to them through the Holy Spirit.

SURRENDER

I really don't like the word *surrender*. Mostly I put surrender in the context of defeat. The picture comes to mind of some old World War II footage of a soldier pointing his weapon down in some rat hole. Then these poor, half-starved enemies emerge all boney-looking and confused. They raise their hands in the air, put them on the top of their heads, and then lie facedown on the ground and say, "We surrender."

I have to know the "me" God created me to be, not the person I desire to be, but the God "me." Just like Jesus, I have to surrender. I can't walk in my desire. The Bible calls that walking in the flesh—he who walks in the flesh will carry out the desires of the flesh.[7] That means I'm being my own "me" and not God's "me."

> Those who live according to the sinful nature [flesh] have their minds set on what that nature desires; but those who live in accordance with the Spirit have their minds set on what the Spirit desires. The mind of sinful man is death, but the mind controlled by the Spirit is life and peace; the sinful mind [governed by the flesh] is hostile to God. It does not submit to God's law, nor can it do so. Those controlled by the sinful nature cannot please God.[8]

Jesus said, "If you refuse to take up your cross and follow me, you are not worthy of being mine."[9] I have to walk in surrender to the will and voice of the Father just as Jesus did. And honestly I'm glad the Bible described Jesus as "the author and finisher of our faith, who for the joy that was set before Him endured the cross, despising the shame, and has sat down at the right hand of the throne of God."[10]

At times being the God "me" is really difficult. But you can be encouraged that you are not alone when you feel that way. Jesus felt the same way about the cross.

Paul also said that if I walk in the Spirit, I will do what the Spirit desires.[11] That is where I have to be. That's the God "me"! That's when I'm listening and following the Spirit of God.

We have a choice. We can choose not to follow the voice of God through the Spirit, but then we will never know our real place as a child of God. "Those who are led by the Spirit of God are sons of God."[12]

If I am not God's "me," then I will not understand or be able to function in the other parts of the body of Christ—His church. If I'm not the right "me," I will not function properly in the "we" or "us"!

The church is the bride of Christ—His body, the earthly holder of His power and glory. The mechanism God planned, purposed, and empowered to finish the mission He started was the church.

Too often we ask the wrong question: What am I being given? No! The right question we should be asking is: What am I giving?

We don't look for a fish; we need to look for and learn to use a net. Jesus said we should be "fishers of men." Me, I must catch others in my craveable net! Here's the deal: What God has told us to do and what has to get done, we will never get it done on our own. We need the church.

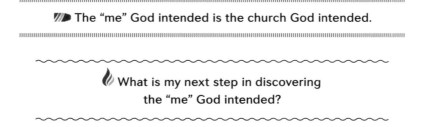

The "me" God intended is the church God intended.

What is my next step in discovering
the "me" God intended?

13

HE LOOKED FOR HIS "WE"

He called His disciples to Himself; and from them He chose twelve.[1]

 Jesus's plan was to give His power and vision away.

EVER BEEN THE last one picked for a team? You know that feeling of standing there saying to yourself, "Please pick me so I don't throw up on myself from embarrassment."

That's a horrible feeling. But if you are ever in the place of the one doing the choosing, you know the other side of trying to put together a winning team around you.

Jesus needed a winning team. He was the catalyst, the cornerstone, the Alpha and Omega. He had the first word, and He will have the last. But He had a job, a mission, and a personal destiny to fulfill. The only hope for the future of mankind was Jesus fulfilling His destiny.

Jesus knew that if He didn't give the vision and power away, the plan of kingdom growth would stall out in Jerusalem after His departure.

THEN JESUS WENT LOOKING FOR HIS "WE"

In one of Jesus's last prayers He looked back over His life and said, "You have given Me followers from this world." Think about this for a minute. Who gave Jesus the followers? The Father gave Jesus the followers. Jesus said, "No one can come to Me unless the Father who sent Me draws him."[2] In other words, for those followers to come to Jesus, the Father had to draw them to Jesus. And the Father uses the Spirit to draw people to Jesus. The Father also used the Spirit of God to speak to the hearts of men. Jesus had to listen to the Father to know who His real followers were.

These guys were pivotal. They were the ones chosen for "special forces" training. They were going to learn the necessary skills and attitudes to lead an advancement team. This team would infiltrate every corner of the globe with the power of a craveable kingdom.

Jesus prayed, fasted, and then asked the Father who His followers were:

> Now it came to pass in those days that He went out to the mountain to pray, and continued all night in prayer to God. And when it was day, He called His disciples to Himself; and from them He chose twelve whom He also named apostles.[3]

Then He went out the next day, found them, and invited them to join Him on His journey. They were the ones prepared to hear His invitation. If not, I don't believe they would have followed! The Spirit had prepared their hearts for the words of Jesus.

Why do you think the fishermen immediately left their nets and followed Jesus? Don't you think this is kind of strange? Even though Jesus had a reputation, they probably had never met Him. If Jesus had asked those in the next boat, they would have said no. The Father had already sent the Spirit before Him to prepare them. So when they were called, they were ready.

Do you know how important it is to hear God's voice? If you don't use your ears, your eyes will never work.

Jesus said, "I only do what I see my Father doing."[4] In other words, the Father and Spirit knew who was ready and who had been prepared to follow Jesus.

We need to understand that God has followers for us. Yeah, it may not sound like we've had our slice of humble pie when we say this, but it's true. God has people around us whom we'll come in contact with and who are meant to follow us. They will follow us and the Christ in us.

Jesus told His followers what the Father had told Him, and they accepted it. If you can grasp the truth that the Father is working all around you by the power of the Spirit and that He is preparing some to listen to what the Father has told you, then you will be eager to listen to the voice of the Father. Jesus understood that He couldn't just go out and randomly grab somebody. He had to listen to the Father to know whom He should invest in.

Now once Jesus understood who those followers were, He didn't just send them a letter or text message that He wanted to meet them. No! He initiated the process by going to find them.

Jesus was always looking. He was always listening and looking at the same time. "Father, what about this one, that one?" But if He wasn't listening to the Father, His eyes would not have seen the right people!

The Spirit of God is working in people your life touches. I like to call it "following the plow." Those who have experience in farming, of which I have none, will understand this. Don't get me wrong. I love the peanuts, okra, and butterbeans that come from farms. And farmers are the hardest-working people in the world, but I am not a farmer.

Although it was against my will, however, I did help my dad in the garden when I was a boy. I found out that after the ground had been left to itself—through ice, rain, and sun—it had to be plowed before you could plant the seeds. If not, the seeds would not take root and produce a crop.

So many times we don't take the time to listen to God before we start investing our time and life into people. Their hearts are hard, and we may have missed the ones ready to receive what they would see and hear. We need to follow the plow of the Spirit. Every day we are looking to initiate in the life of someone else. The question is, whom should you invest in? God has people ready, and we need to listen.

We see this principle put into practice during Paul's visit to the city of Philippi. A wealthy businesswoman named Lydia crossed the line of faith and surrendered her life to Christ. There are some details that help us see how God's Spirit plowed the ground to make it all happen. First we see that there were two other places Paul tried to go before he ended in Philippi speaking with a group of praying women including Lydia.

Paul's team was "forbidden by the Holy Spirit to preach the word in Asia," and then "they tried to go into Bithynia, but the Spirit did not permit them."[5] What? Paul, Timothy, and Silas were doing the right thing for all the right reasons. They were going to preach the truth! Why would God's Spirit possibly stop them? The answer was pretty simple. The timing was not right because the plowing of the Holy Spirit was not done. God was at work through His Spirit in Philippi.

Look at this awesome picture of being in the right place at the right time with the right person. Paul was redirected to Lydia, and "the Lord opened her heart to heed the things spoken by Paul."[6] She became the first convert to Christ in a brand-new church in Philippi. And the Holy Spirit kept plowing until He got to me!

Paul explained it this way: "Now we have received, not the spirit of the world, but the Spirit who is from God, that we might know the things that have been freely given to us by God."[7] The context of this specific verse is referring to spiritual gifts. But I also believe it is speaking to the fact that anything God gives us, the Spirit tells us about so that we can know what belongs to us. That includes the people God has given us to impact for Him. Just as God has given Jesus followers, the Father has given followers to you. Take the time to hear from God about who you should invest your life in.

Paul said, "Follow my example, as I follow the example of Christ."[8]

That's kind of hard to tell someone, isn't it? "Follow me." Another translation says, "Imitate me, just as I also imitate Christ."[9] We try to talk ourselves out of the implications of such a command, even resorting to false humility. If we can't say "mimic" me as a Christ-follower (the original word translated "imitate" or "follow" is "mimic"), why not? We need to ask God why and let Him make the necessary life corrections in us. We need to recognize our sin and repent.

Why do we say, "Come hear me, and go follow Jesus; come do this Bible study with me, and go follow Jesus; come go to church with me, and go follow Jesus." We have lost the weight needed to tell someone, "If you want to know what Jesus looks like, just live with me for a while. If you want to know what love, acceptance, and loyalty are, come spend time with me."

Jesus knew He was just one man; He couldn't reach the world, and He didn't! What He did was strategically equip and empower His "we." His followers the Father gave Him were critical to the mission to reach the world. He did life with those guys, ate with them, cried with them, and prayed with them.

Jesus established an effective form of "organizing" His circle or His "we." He selected His circle from the crowd, and then prioritized those in His circle.

He influenced 12.

He invested in 3.

He was intimate with 1.

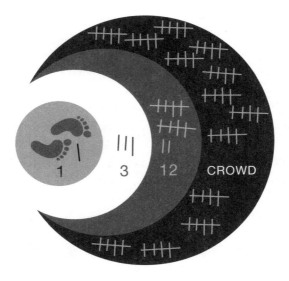

Remember, Jesus was all man. He was limited in strength and emotional will. And we all know people; even those whom we love and care for can be draining! These guys who were with Jesus seemed to really take it out of Him.

He influenced all twelve of His followers. They ate together and spent time talking around the grilling of meat and fish. They walked together, knew each other's families, and probably kidded each other about the lengths of the other's robe. But it's difficult, well, let's say humanly impossible to be very close to twelve people at the same time! Jesus couldn't even do it.

He invested more in three of them than He did the others. Peter, James, and John were the three guys Jesus invested the most in. When you invest in someone, it takes a lot out of you. You pour a lot into someone you are investing in.

Jesus took these guys almost everywhere He went. He even excluded the other nine from some "private showings." When Jesus raised the little girl from the dead, only Peter, James, and John were allowed in. When He was transfigured on a mountain, only those three were allowed to "go up" with Jesus and behold such a sight!

Then there was the intimate one—the apostle whom Jesus loved—John. John was allowed to rest on the chest of Jesus. And when others had a sensitive question to ask, "Who is going to betray the Lord?", they turned to John and said, "Hey, bud, you're His fave. You ask Him."

We all have a "crowd" that we have an opportunity to impact. We have people close enough to us to be drawn in the kingdom by our craveability. Some will enter in; many will not. But we always have to listen for opportunities and not miss any!

Paul said he was free from the blood of all men:

> Now I know that none of you among whom I have gone about preaching the kingdom will ever see me again. Therefore, I declare to you today that I am innocent of the blood of all men. For I have not hesitated to proclaim to you the whole will of God.[10]

I believe Paul followed the example of Jesus. He heard the voice of God, and he knew the followers God had for him. And Paul said he never left one. He impacted, initiated, and invested in everyone whom God had for him, and he felt free from the blood of all men.

Jesus said the same thing. He said He didn't lose one! "I have manifested Your name to the men whom You have given Me out of the world. They were Yours, You gave them to Me, and they have kept Your word."[11]

Let me challenge you: in your life, where you are right now? You may be thinking, "I can't help anybody. I need help myself." God's wisdom from the Book of Proverbs says, "He who refreshes others will himself be refreshed."[12]

You can bring people into the kingdom no matter where you are. Whether you've been a part of the kingdom a week or twenty years, God has people He wants you to impact. Here is how God's Word explains it: "Anyone who claims to be intimate with God ought to live the same kind of life Jesus lived."[13]

So if you belong to Christ, you must live as Jesus lived. You cannot be a true Christ-follower and not feel the weight of this.

God made Jesus's followers ready to say yes to Him.

What did Jesus do that I can do?

14

I LOOK FOR MY "WE"

And the LORD God said, "It is not good that man should be alone."[1]

⬤ God created me to be with a "we."

I REMEMBER HEARING A group of kids in high school saying things like, "We are going to the game," or "We are going out to eat and see a movie." *We* is one of the most powerful words in the English language. I remember saying to myself, "Me wanna we. Me need a we!" Every one of us who is a "me" needs a "we." It is not good for us to be alone!

That group eventually offered me a spot in their "we," and it was in that "we" that this "me" found Jesus! I experienced the power of being accepted and part of something bigger than myself.

One of the reasons prisoners are put in solitary confinement is so they can lose their minds in there! People aren't wired to be alone! It is *not* good for us to be alone. Remember the movie *Castaway?* Tom Hanks was alone and went crazy talking to his homemade volleyball friend, Wilson.

Even God has a "we": "Let us make man in our image."[2]

Jesus set a great example for us to follow, but I think it was a template and not a "magical" combination. He wanted us to see and understand our own requirements and limitations. We are all wired differently, but we are required to carry out His mission together.

> *By myself I can do nothing…*I seek not to please myself but him who sent me.[3]

The Father knew Jesus had to have others to accomplish the mission. Jesus could not have done it by Himself. We certainly can't!

Every "me" needs a "we." We can't do what God has required or called us to do alone. All of us are better than some of us.

I think we need two circles in our "we." One is comprised of those inside the church—those I'm practicing the "one anothers" and doing life with. Let's call this one our "church" circle:

1. Influence (12)

2. Invest (3)

3. Intimate (1)

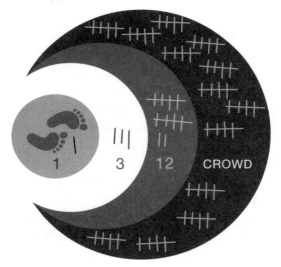

I have some men in my life who have kept me going when I felt I couldn't keep going. They hold my hands up in the hard times. They are like my "special forces" team who guards and protects me.

This circle must be chosen carefully and prayerfully because they matter! "Give me a team of people who know how to watch, wait, listen, people who fast, pray and surrender rather than always trying to take control."[4]

Don't you want somebody to tell you if you have a spinach leaf on your front tooth? I sure do. Why? Because I don't want to walk around looking like an idiot. I don't want everybody afraid to look at me, fearing they will either laugh or hurl in my face. We need people close enough to us tell us what they see.

The other "we" is comprised mostly of those outside or newly inside. This is the circle I do life with. For them I want to demonstrate a high level of craveability, showing them that Jesus is the real deal.

And these two circles should and must merge at times! I need my "in we" to help me win my "out we." That's why Jesus always sent those with Him, His "in we," out two by two. They needed one another. We should never do ministry alone. Have you ever noticed that whether it is Barnabas, Silas, John Mark, or Timothy, Paul never did ministry alone? He always had someone with him.

BEGIN WITH A CIRCLE

We all have circles. Just look where you are in a Christian atmosphere, and *bam!* Draw a circle around yourself. Look for those you migrate to and have chemistry with. That is your circle.

Now I know it's admirable to think that anybody will fit into our circle. We are all accepting and would love to extend our energy and love to anyone. But that's really not reality. The fact is, we simply will not grow close to someone we don't like! Yes, we have to love everybody, but we certainly won't like everybody.

When I say "like," I mean the person has qualities, traits, and similarities to you that make you want to be with them. You're not with them out of obligation or because of ministry. People in your circle are those you enjoy spending time with.

Now there are others we need to give time and energy to whom we don't really love being with. They need us in their lives, and we need relational space for them. Yes, we will give love, energy, time, and acceptance to them, but there must be a circle, a group, or our own "we" that fuels our passions and concerns for others in order for us to be fully effective.

GROWS INTO A COMMUNITY

Now a circle must continue to move and grow, not necessarily in number (even though that is desirable and necessary with time), but in trust, transparency, and influence with each other.

There has to be a "growing into" process before a community of believers can truly demonstrate to those on the outside the real love of God. "By this all will know that you are My disciples, if you have love for one another."[5]

As real relationship takes place, this grows a circle into a community.

A *community* is defined as "a group of people with a common characteristic or interest living together within a larger society."[6] The key here is a common characteristic. The circle, as it grows into a community, understands their mission in the beginning, but over time it becomes a part of them as a group. They become co-owners of the mission. And they want to be together! This is absolutely vital.

We can't look at this as some satisfying of a feeling of responsibility. But community must be an intentional life choice and mindset revelation. Also included in the process is the transformation of habit, action, and thought. A circle morphs into an attitude of "this is who I am; I am a vital part of the lives of these others."

GOES OUTWARD AS A CRAVEABLE COMMUNITY

What begins as a circle should mature into a community. Our circles are actual communities. And these need to be "craveable communities."

We need each other to reach others.

We can't carry out the mission without followers. That's why Jesus prayed for His followers; He knew He couldn't do what the Father told Him to do without them. And we have to pray for ours; we can't carry out our mission without "Spirit-plowed" followers. We have already talked about "the weight of the what." Now let's talk about the "the who" factor.

When we "invest" in the lives of those in our circles, it's important to know...

Who are they?

Investing is a tricky business. In Scripture "seed" is referred to as the kingdom as well as money and financial resources. Consider this: Would you invest your money without listening to someone who knows the best place for the highest return? We invest looking for the greatest return on our kingdom investment!

"Me" always needs a "we." It's not good that man should be alone!

> We loved you so much that we shared with you not only God's Good News but our own lives, too.[7]

> As the Father loved Me, I also have loved you.... This is My commandment, that you love one another as I have loved you. Greater love has no one than this, than to lay down one's life for his friends.[8]

Honestly, I'm glad Jesus said I'm to love my "friends" like that and not everyone! We do have to love everyone, but we can only lay down our life for those we do life with! So we need to hear from God as Jesus did about His "we"—His 12-3-1.

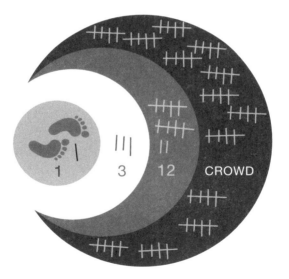

I think this is where the raw power of the church is: in our "we." These are close, caring, and daring units that can move powerfully to impact the lives of people.

> Let us be concerned for one another, to help one another to show love and to do good. Let us not give up the habit of meeting together.... Instead, let us encourage one another all the more.[9]

In our "we" is where we practice the "one anothers" found in the New Testament. It's how we learn to love, serve, honor, and care for others.

We live in a culture that sucks all of our concern for others out of us with busyness. Have you ever heard about someone and thought, "I don't really care right now"? I have done that! There are too many things going on in my life at the moment. I have no emotional energy left to give away.

Every season of life seems too busy—from school, to dating, to marriage, to raising kids, to work, to retirement, and then we move away. Busy is the consistent thread through every season of life. That means the chances to really do kingdom work and affect the lives of people are just slipping away in the midst of our busyness. If we are too busy for "we" time, then we are just too busy for the kingdom.

We need help to love. Some people are hard to love. That's why we need "we" people around us. I have needed help to know how to love my wife, my kids, and some "hard-to-love" friends.

> Every day the Lord saved people, and they were added to the group.[10]

I remember telling a couple of guys I'm close to (on different occasions) how they were really messing up with their wives. They really didn't love their spouses as they should. To one of them I finally had to say, "Listen, man, if you don't straighten up, I'm going to kick your butt!" Now, I don't recommend you going around and threatening to kick other men's butts; however, I believe I was about to deliver a righteous whooping.

You can't have that kind of "help" from somebody unless you are close enough to earn the right to speak that kind of truth to a person. He needed it! And on many occasions others close to me have told me hard things I didn't want to hear but sure needed it.

WE ARE CALLED TO LOVE ONE ANOTHER

> A new commandment I give to you, that you love one another; as I have loved you, that you also love one another. By this all will know that you are My disciples, if you have love for one another.[11]

Jesus said, "Love as I have loved." He's talking about the people in your circle.

Jesus was talking about loving your "we"—your circle of close friends or group. There's no way to love as Jesus loved without an investment of time.

In our "we" we still have to be craveable. And our craveability is what others closest to us...

+ See
+ Hear
+ Experience

Part of what we are supposed to be doing is helping those close to us follow and be like Jesus. And those close to us are not going to give any weight to our encouragement, correction, or input if they don't have a good perception of us!

Remember, perception is king!

Those who are the closet to me should have the best perception of me. I know, most of us are afraid to let the real us come through; we don't want others to see all our nastiness and crud. But they have it too. And if you will help me get rid of my crud without judging but just loving me, then I will help you get rid of your nastiness.

I don't know about you, but some of the nastiest, meanest people I've ever met were "Christians." I mean like big nasty! And most are mean and nasty in the "name of Jesus." They think they are doing the right thing by telling others lies and gossiping about things they don't know. They try and spoil others' reputations just so they can feel better about themselves. That does incredible damage to the kingdom, because those on the outside see all that junk! They hear it at work, home, and play. They see fellow believers tearing one another up, not loving one another as Jesus did, and their takeaway from all that as observers is, "Christians are terrible! Why would I want to be like them?"

The life and love we demonstrate, that which others are allowed to see, hear, and experience, has to be craveable. If not, they will run away—far, far away.

We have to be together. We have to meet and do life together. This is done with a smaller setting and circle of people.

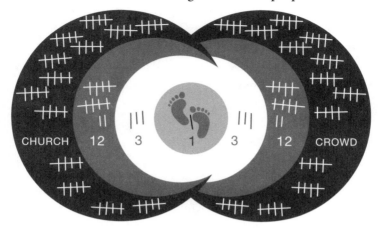

Let me tell you another reason it's almost impossible to be craveable to those outside the kingdom if we aren't in a "we." Because lonely people are not happy people! I don't care if you think, "I like being by myself." That's a lie! God created us to be "people." If you have had a bad experience and now you're bitter, that does not mean you don't need community. You may have trouble trusting, so you just stay by yourself in fear of being hurt again. You need to get that right, because Satan loves it when you're lonely.

Lonely, loner people aren't craveable, because they aren't happy! I don't find miserable people good company! There are times when you have to help those who are miserable. We minister, love, and care for them at Cornerstone. But if you're outside the kingdom, miserable, lonely people aren't going to look irresistible to anybody!

It's not good for us to be alone!

It's important that we love the people around us and that we have them there. That's why Jesus prayed in John 17 that we'd be one with other believers just as He and the Father are one. He prayed we'd be close to each other, invest in each other, and do life together in unity.

> Carry each other's burdens, and in this way you will fulfill the law of Christ.[12]

I must be craveable to those inside
and outside the kingdom.

What about me is unattractive to Christ-followers?

15

HE LOOKED FOR HIS "US"

*There were also women looking on from a distance...they
would follow Him and help Him.*[1]

⬤ Jesus did life and ministry with an "us" (church).

MANY HANDS MAKE light work." That's an old saying
I've heard for years. It means the more people we have
helping us, the lighter the burden on a few. That makes
a lot of sense to me, because the more who get involved, the more
that gets done.

When Jesus picked His "winning team" of twelve, He knew He
would need more than that to complete the mission. He needed a
lot of help, and He got it! He had a multitude of followers who were
far beyond just the original Twelve. They were vital in helping Him
and then launching the church after His ascension.

Jesus had more than just His close circle of followers; He also had
a crowd of believers (like a foreshadowing of the soon-coming church).

MANY

Jesus knew He had to start with "me," then He needed a "we," but
He also needed an "us." He had a big "us." A lot people believed in
Jesus. They helped Him on His journey and with His ministry. In
fact, Jesus called His "we." Remember? Jesus said, "Come to me, *all*
of you who are weary and carry heavy burdens, and I will give you
rest."[2]

"Come to me, all..." Jesus understood how important it was for

100

Him to have a "we." He knew how important it was for Him to do life and ministry with not just Himself and His close circle but also with many people.

MIXED

You could see the extent of His "us" when Jesus would move around from place to place. The Bible says many who believed in Him went with Him. When you think about it, that is a natural occurrence. Jesus wouldn't have had a very fruitful life if all He had to show for it was twelve empowered blue-collar guys. No. He had religious leaders, people of prominence, middle class, and lowly. A vast multiethnic mix of believers composed Jesus's "us."

Women were some of His strongest supporters. They cared for Him, helped support Him financially, and often went with Him impacting cities and villages. In fact, women got to the tomb first to notice that Jesus was no longer buried. It wasn't one of Jesus's disciples or His brothers who got to the tomb first. Jesus attracted such a mixed crowd that someone (a woman) who was often rejected and looked down upon in society witnessed the greatest event in history!

MULTIPLIED

Those who believed in Jesus would go out and tell others about Him. Their personal testimony of how they came to know Him was convincing. Friends and family became believers because they saw the incredible change in the lives of the people closest to them transformed by Christ. These followers of Jesus saw something in Him that got them excited enough to go out and bring others to Him. He was perceived in such a way that His followers multiplied because of their passion for following Him. Jesus was worth talking about, and they did.

Jesus needed the "we" (disciples) to build the "us."

How am I encouraging others to build the "us"?

16

I LOOK FOR MY "US"

I will build my church, and all the powers of hell will not conquer it.[1]

 The "us" (church) gathered is a big threat to Satan.

"I DON'T NEED TO go to church to be a Christian." Oh, my, how many times have I heard that? And I agree. Are you surprised? You certainly don't have to "go to" church, but you sure need to be the church and an active part of it. You do not need the church to be a Christian but certainly to succeed as one!

The corporate gathering of the local church is the representation of the bride of Christ in her fullest power and glory. The church gathered is the biggest threat to the kingdom of darkness that could ever be imagined. Satan hates and despises the local church. It's the thing all Satan's power cannot prevail against.

If I'm not a part of that gathering, I open myself up to so many assaults. I'm not under the protection of the corporate church gathering. I'm not a part of the very tool God is going to use to take His message beyond where we are and our generation to the entire world. If I'm not a part of the bride of Christ, it's like someone telling me they really like me, but they don't care to know my wife. That hurts Christ and hurts our ability to grow in Him. And without the church and my corresponding growth in Christ I cannot possibly become craveable to people in my world. My spiritual or moral life is all about the great choices I make. My connection with the local church helps people see I am not all about me but about God and His purpose in the world.

MOVING

"Move or die. Move or die," is heard often from the corner in a MMA (mixed martial arts) fight. You see, in MMA, they know if you just stand still, you are a dead target for your opponent.

You hear so many people saying, "I don't have to be in the church to be a Christian." That's so right! You don't. But to be a victorious Christian, you have to be!

The church of "us" is comprised of "mes" and "wes." But it all starts with each of us individually understanding that part of our mission is to move. We can't stand still in our walk with God. I'm not talking about not "being still" before God or taking needed rests and escapes. Those disconnect times are a vital part of us moving with God. I'm talking about our desire to move forward in the kingdom and in Christ. I'm talking about our devotion to help others do so as well.

The church of "us" can never stop moving forward. The way the "us" church keeps moving is by being the catalyst of making mature Christ-followers. The corporate body is where the fullness of leadership is displayed and employed.

> Now these are the gifts Christ gave to the church: the apostles, the prophets, the evangelists, and the pastors and teachers. Their responsibility is to equip God's people to do his work and build up the church.[2]

A church should be moving people to maturity. And since we are supposed to constantly add new people to the kingdom, this process is ongoing and never ending.

> This will continue until we all come to such unity in our faith and knowledge of God's Son that we will be mature in the Lord, measuring up to the full and complete standard of Christ.[3]

MIXED

Every tribe, nation, and tongue...that's whom we have to reach with the love of Jesus. It's not enough for us to stay in our holy huddle of people who look, talk, and act just like us. No. We're called to do what Jesus did. We're called to move beyond our comfort zone and reach out to every nation, tribe, and tongue. Every people group deserves to hear about the life-changing message of Jesus. And every people group around us deserves to hear it from us.

We have to have a mixed "we." Let's face it: everywhere else we go has different races and ethnicities represented. Why can't that be in our churches as well? Why can't we have that in our homes?

> The way God designed our bodies is a model for understanding our lives together as a church: every part dependent on every other part.[4]

> The believers had a single purpose.[5]

> Every kingdom divided against itself is headed for destruction, and no city or house divided against itself will stand.[6]

MULTIPLYING

> The believers had a single purpose and went to the temple every day. They were joyful and humble as they ate at each other's homes and shared their food. At the same time, they praised God and had the good will of all the people. Every day the Lord saved people, and they were added to the group.[7]

The church of us, the local gathering of the body and bride of Christ—this is the holder of the "manifold wisdom of God."

Pastor Mark Driscoll and Dr. Gerry Breshears, in their book *Doctrine*, offer this helpful biblical definition of the local church:

> The local church is a community of regenerated believers who confess Jesus Christ as Lord. In obedience to Scripture they organize under qualified leadership, gather regularly for preaching and worship, observe the biblical sacraments of baptism and communion, are unified by the Spirit, are disciplined for holiness, and scatter to fulfill the great commandment and the great commission as missionaries to the world for God's glory and their joy.[8]

> So that if I am delayed, you will know how people must conduct themselves in the household of God. This is the church

of the living God, which is the pillar and foundation of the truth.[9]

Jesus (the one we call Justus) also sends his greetings. These are the only Jewish believers among my co-workers; they are working with me here for the Kingdom of God. And what a comfort they have been.[10]

I challenge you to pray this prayer:

Father, You have given me followers. Tell me their names, and I will find them, live with them, love them, and they will accept it. Open my eyes, speak to me, and show me which ones You need me to befriend, love, and accept unconditionally, so that I can help them find, follow, and be like You.

⫸ If I am not in the "us," I am not in the movement.

🔥 How can I support the "us" on a deeper level?

PART 4

CRAVEABLE LOVING

Then Jesus, looking at him, loved him.[1]

I DON'T KNOW OF anything more powerful and feeding to the life of another person than unconditional love and acceptance—the kind of love and acceptance that doesn't judge or juke, the authentic love and acceptance that invests and gives and doesn't put a "return to sender" sticker on it.

Real love is craveable! People love to be loved. It's written in their DNA by God's own hand. If we understand that, we hold the key to the kingdom and have the power to see countless people come to know Jesus through the actions and heart of love. As a matter of fact, not loving other people is a pretty serious matter with God.

> And even as they did not like to retain God in their knowledge, God gave them over to a debased mind, to do those things which are not fitting…untrustworthy, *unloving*, unforgiving, unmerciful…*those who practice such things are deserving of death.*[2]

Now, I didn't write that; God did, and that's some serious stuff right there. Honestly that really scares me. You see, all those things (the list is actually longer) are totally against the character of God, and we are supposed to be like God in such things, including love. Being unloving is so far removed from where God wants us to be!

Our lives must reflect the heart of the Father, and His heart is full of love. Jesus's sure did…

17

HE LOVED "OUT OF BOUNDS"

*God has shown me that I should no longer think
of anyone as impure or unclean.*[1]

⬤ Jesus hung out with those nobody else wanted.

BEING OR FEELING unloved is a very painful and lonely place. Most of us experience it during some point in our lives, and it can cause incredible damage. We not only feel worthless, but we also feel hopeless. This is a terrible place to be—yet Jesus was drawn to people there.

Love is a huge investment. I'm not talking about just being loving. We must be loving to be craveable. But I'm talking about an intentional investment—real love, where you know that what you're doing is pouring into someone's life. Jesus loved His followers, and He loved His friends.

Jesus was a friend to the sinner. In other words, He befriended and loved not only those who followed Him but also those who were far from Him. He was...

A FRIEND TO THOSE "OUT OF BOUNDS"

How many of you have ever played or watched a football game? When you are playing football, you see people on the sidelines or in the stands. Those people are "out of bounds." They are off the field; they aren't on the field, so they aren't in the game or subject to the rules on the field.

Jesus loved those who were "out of bounds."

Who are they?

You know, the ones who are untouchable whom you're not supposed to be with? The ones you're criticized for if you're friends with them. They're too rich or they're too poor, or maybe they have the wrong sexual orientation. You're not supposed to know their music or appreciate their art. You're not supposed to hang out with them. The ones who are out of bounds are the ones who Jesus went to—and who came to Him.

> The Son of Man came and ate and drank. They said, "See! He eats too much and likes wine. He is a friend of men who gather taxes and of sinners!"[2]

Jesus was their friend.

Now isn't that a crazy idea. Make friends, real friends, with those outside the kingdom of God. The picture here is not of a casual friend but a close friend who was not only acquainted with "men who gather taxes and of sinners" but also who was loved by them and He loved them back. "A friend," as described by the wisest man that ever lived, "loves at all times."[3]

That doesn't mean that all these people Jesus was friends with, who were out of bounds, met with His approval. We love at all times, but that doesn't mean we agree with or approve of their lifestyle or choices.

There is a huge difference between acceptance and approval. Jesus didn't approve of Zacchaeus's thievery or the Samaritan woman's immorality. What He did was accept and love them.

We have to learn from Jesus how to be friends with others, accepting and loving them but not always approving of their actions or habits.

Remember, "out of bounds" people aren't on the field! Only when you are on the field are you subject to its requirements. So as we are on the field, engaged in kingdom activities, we can't throw rocks of judgment and criticism at those not on the field! When we come into a relationship with Jesus, we are "put on the field." We are on the field with others who have also come to know Jesus. Now, all those who have yet to know Jesus are off the field. They are "out of bounds."

Jesus said, "It is the sick who need what I have."[4] Those who are on the field don't need what I have, so I have to go out of bounds to reach the people who need me. And this is what I find interesting…

The religious "leaders" then hated Jesus for being with them.

They were telling Jesus, "You're not just hanging out with these guys, but You're also being a friend to these people." But Jesus came "to seek and to save that which was lost."[5] So if everyone who was "in bounds" is found, where was He going to find those who were lost and sick? Out of bounds!

And that's where Jesus was. He was in places where others thought He shouldn't be. I would imagine He was up in their houses eating, drinking, and laughing. The point is, Jesus was being real with those He needed to impact. He was where they were, just doing real life with them.

This was the process of Him impacting, initiating, and investing in those who needed the kingdom. And guess what? The process worked!

These lost and needy people loved Jesus! They found Him irresistible. They couldn't get enough of Him. They followed Him, stalked Him, spied on Him, and even committed felonies, like breaking and entering, just to get close to Him!

They were so unlike the "religious leaders" of the day, who hated Jesus because He wasn't doing things their way. They questioned Jesus, "Don't You know what the law says?" Now what they meant by the law was the man-made ideals they came up with, which really weren't in Scripture, but they wanted them to be. They were constantly coming up to Him saying, "Well, the law says…," and Jesus's response was like, "Dude, I wrote the Bible. You guys have added a bunch of nonsense to Scripture that I didn't put in there. And now *you* want to tell *Me* I'm doing something wrong by quoting Me something *you* wrote."

Somebody will say, "I know a lot of people out of bounds in that strip club down the street. I know there are a lot of people in there who don't know Jesus. I'm going to be a strip-club evangelist!" God will never tell you to sin in order to fulfill His commandment. Now, I'm going to be honest with you. There are a lot of you who may have a broader definition of what sin is than me. In that lie a lot of problems with people. Some still have a religious mind-set and add standards and regulations that are not clearly laid out in Scripture.

I know a fellow who was known as one of the "baddest" dudes in my town. After he found Christ, he went back in the bars to talk with the only people he knew—those "out of bounds." Some of his "out of bounds" friends now come to church with him. He asked me if he was doing all right. I told him to go and be blessed; he was really doing it like Jesus did. Some of us should follow his example.

Sadly most of us spend the majority of our time on the field with our fellow players and neglect those still off the field. We will even judge those who leave the field to recruit and spend time with those in the stands trying to get them on the field. But that is whom the apostle Paul said we needed to be with:

> I wrote to you in my epistle not to keep company with sexually immoral people. Yet I certainly did not mean with the sexually immoral people of this world, or with the covetous, or extortioners, or idolaters, since then you would need to go out of the world.[6]

Then Paul said, "You know, you can't hang out with someone who says they are a Christian and does these things. But we need to be with those who do these things and aren't believers!"

Some of you are spending time with people "out of bounds" but are not telling them about Jesus. Some of you are not spending time with anyone "out of bounds." You've been saved for 106 years, and everything you do is in the church. You haven't been a friend to a sinner since you were in preschool.

My wife, Georgie, was in her early twenties when God spoke to her about becoming friends with a lady named Kathy. Up to this point in her life Georgie had only been hanging around people "in bounds." So this was her first "out of bounds" friend! She recalls having an overpowering feeling that their friendship was going to make some great impact; she could see the Spirit of God working in Kathy's life.

After a year or so Kathy had a crisis in her life and turned to Georgie for an answer. "You have a peace, a power, something that is craveable." This led to the opportunity to lead Kathy into a relationship with her Creator!

God has called you to go to the "out of bounds" places to the "out of bounds" people and reach those who are off the field. Pray that God will send you someone who needs to see and hear the gospel message. When was the last time you prayed that? Sometimes we pray for people to get saved, but we aren't willing to go where they are and be with them. People respond to people who genuinely care about them.

If we're more concerned about what church folks think than being somewhere that's "out of bounds" or being with someone who is "out of bounds," then truly we are straight-up Pharisees. We don't understand what it's like to "walk as Jesus walked."

〃▶ Jesus invested in those who were farthest from Him.

〰〰〰〰〰〰〰〰〰〰〰〰〰〰〰〰〰〰〰〰〰〰〰

◊ How can I make a new connection with
someone far from Him this week?

〰〰〰〰〰〰〰〰〰〰〰〰〰〰〰〰〰〰〰〰〰〰〰

18

I LOVE "OUT OF BOUNDS"

If you only love the lovable, do you expect a pat on
the back? Run-of-the-mill sinners do that.[1]

⬤ I need to be craveable to people "out of bounds."

SOME PEOPLE ARE hard to love. It is a natural instinct to love those who love us. We feel an obligation to show love to someone who has loved us, but to truly love the person who just doesn't seem to deserve or appreciate the attention or love we show is a real easy situation to bail out on.

"I truly want people to spend time working on their relationship with God. I just want them to do it by taking the time to care about the person standing right in front of them"[2]...because He sent His Son to die for them and Jesus gave His life for them. Jesus gave an example of how to live, going after those who really mattered. He explained His mission (and ours): "For the Son of Man has come to seek and to save that which was lost."[3] Our mission is to impact those who are lost, least, lonely, and lowly. Those who no one else wants to touch are the ones we should crave. You see, as we become more craveable to those around us, in turn we crave to be with them.

But our mission is a life journey, not a destination with many steps to take and places to go along the way. It's not just those "out of bounds" whom we are to impact on our journey. It's every new person we meet with each new step. It's every person in the place along the way, like friends, coworkers, neighbors, spouses, and children.

114

Can I be honest with you? Some of you are really weird. And you know what? God made you that way. There are other weird people like you, which only you can impact. God uniquely gifted you. There are people in your life God divinely planned for you to bring into the kingdom, and it grieves His heart when you don't take the time to ask whom He's working in. And if you don't care about who He has planned for you, then you're missing your responsibility to reflect.

Jesus explained the principles of the kingdom in the story of the seed scatter in Mark 4. In this passage seed falls on different types of ground. Some never amount to anything, some are just short lived, and others produce a terrific harvest—some thirty, sixty, even one hundredfold return!

Our patience for being around religious, self-righteous, and judgmental Pharisees is short (only as we become less like them). The word *seek* is not a passive word. Lost people are not our hobby or special prayer emphasis one week a year in our local churches. Lost people are our passion, our zeal, and yes, our obsession. We crave to be with them for all the right reasons. The opposite of *seek* is to ignore. Too often, by our actions, we don't seek and save the lost; we ignore and condemn them. But as Paul said in 1 Corinthians 5:9–10, we cannot escape interacting with out-of-bounds people. God is calling us to them.

Luke 10:1–2 says:

> The Lord appointed seventy others also, and sent them two by two before His face into every city and place where He Himself was about to go. Then He said to them, "The harvest truly is great, but the laborers are few; therefore pray the Lord of the harvest to send out laborers into His harvest."

Jesus was saying the "harvest is great." You can't harvest something that is not producing. Only seed that falls on good ground yields a crop. And God is the "Lord of the harvest," so He knows where those are who are close to being ready for the kingdom. He knows the good ground!

God wants specific people in my life
because He wired me to reach them.

What part of my past connects best
with people far from God?

PART 5

CRAVEABLE LIVING

Those who hear and don't act are like those who glance in the mirror, walk away, and two minutes later have no idea who they are, what they look like.[1]

I REMEMBER READING A poem once called "The Dash" by Linda Ellis. I vividly remember the main idea: when we are dead and buried, a tombstone will be placed at the end of the pile of dirt covering our encased remains. It will read something like, "Artie Davis, 1961–2061, the dude who tried to write a book." On that piece of granite the time between the year I was born and the year I died is represented by a simple "dash."

It seems to me that my life should mean more than a short journey between the two hospitals (the one I was born in and the one I die in). That little symbol will represent quite a story for those who knew me. A lifetime of hopes, dreams, failures, victories, relationships, and lost relationships will be seen as nothing but a dash.

> Teach us to realize the brevity of life, so that we may grow in wisdom.[2]

Every day of my life I understand more clearly the power and brilliance packed in this word from God. When we are young, we live fast and hard with a careless attitude about life. We live for the moment. As we get older, we realize the world is bigger than our own lives.

Now I can clearly envision something that humbles me. The world will go on fine without me! People will go on with life after I die. Orangeburg will still be Orangeburg. South Carolina State University will still have classes. And Duke's (the best barbeque in

South Carolina) will not shut down—although they will lose some significant business. The world will remain the same.

Even those closest to me (my wife, children, family, friends, and church), after a time of grieving, will have no other choice but to move on. Hopefully they will have good memories, but they will never see me again until heaven. I will be a goner. So what will I leave? God wants me to approach life with a perspective that is larger than me and larger than today.

There is only one thing that will last beyond that dash for all eternity—the people I helped to find, follow, and be like Jesus.

The people our lives impacted for the kingdom are referred to in Scripture as "true riches." The real treasure, the true value of a life well lived, is proven by the lives that are changed for all eternity as a result of the way we lived while with them.

HE DEMONSTRATED THE POWER OF GOD

Jesus went...and taught the people in the synagogue in a way that amazed them. People were asking, "Where did this man get this wisdom and the power to do these miracles?"[1]

⬤ Most people believed Jesus because
of what they saw Him do.

POWER IS VERY craveable. We are drawn to things and people with power. We like to drop names of the prominent people we may know. We like seeing the power of a fighter jet taking off the deck of an aircraft carrier. We are spellbound when a man has enough power in his hands to rip a large phone book in half or at the influence of an executive to just make a call and secure a job for us.

We all have a natural attraction to supernatural power. When we see or experience something outside of the norm and beyond our abilities, it creates a wonder and excitement that hold our attention and send our imagination into overdrive. God created us like that. He wants us to be in awe of Him and His abilities to manifest and demonstrate His power in us and through us.

One example of the craveability of God's power is in the Book of Acts. A man named Philip was being used by God in Samaria to help people with all kinds of problems. From the paralyzed to the demon possessed, God gave Philip the supernatural power to make them well.

A magician named Simon came to Christ under Philip's influence. Simon was quite impressed with Philip's power-packed ministry. So he did what any normal human being might consider. He offered to buy the power for himself. We pick up on the conversation and watch how Simon really upset Peter for even asking:

> "Let me have this power, too," he exclaimed, "so that when I lay my hands on people, they will receive the Holy Spirit!" But Peter replied, "May your money be destroyed with you for thinking God's gift can be bought!"[2]

Jesus's number-one drawing card was His craveable power. Everywhere He went, people found Him, loved Him, and followed Him. Jesus's ability to draw people to Himself began with a demonstration of the power of God.

Jesus led His followers with great intentionality. He knew that they would be given the task of taking the gospel to the world, and He only had a little over three years to prepare and train them. So He showed them a pattern to follow:

- Demonstrate whom they should believe
- Communicate whom they need to know
- Imitate who they need to be

Knowing whom we are demonstrating, communicating, and emulating is very weighty. Once again we have to understand this is not just a suggestion. I am commanded to live in a way that this "Who" (Jesus) is to be reflected in all I do.

> I have manifested Your name to the men whom You have given Me out of the world. They were Yours, You gave them to Me, and they have kept Your word.[3]

Jesus already showed His followers *whom* they needed to love and impact. He also laid out a process of reaching those God puts in your life to touch. People whom we are reaching out to must know why they should believe us. Jesus answered that by the way He lived in at least three ways.

HE DEMONSTRATED WHOM
THEY SHOULD BELIEVE

> You people must see signs and miracles before you will believe in me.[4]

I love the Gospel of John's account of Jesus taking His followers through this process. After Jesus chose His followers, they followed Him to one of their first stops: a wedding feast. They ran out of wine at this wedding too soon, and Jesus's mom came and told Him the problem.

Jesus gave instruction to fill six water pots with water. Now those pots weren't small cooking pots; those things were huge! After they filled them, "He said to them, 'Draw some out now, and take it to the master of the feast.' And they took it. When the master of the feast had tasted the water that was made wine, and did not know where it came from (but the servants who had drawn the water knew), the master of the feast called the bridegroom. And he said to him, 'Every man at the beginning sets out the good wine, and when the guests have well drunk, then the inferior. You have kept the good wine until now!'"[5]

That was His first "demonstration" of power and glory. Apparently up until now His followers knew they needed to be with Him but hadn't quite made up their minds yet if they were going to stay. John said after Jesus's demonstration, "This beginning of signs Jesus did in Cana of Galilee, and manifested His glory; and His disciples believed in Him."[6]

What, you mean they hadn't believed yet? No, they were following and watching, just not believing yet until they saw. After He demonstrated *why* they should believe in Him, they were like the rest of us: we won't believe someone until we know they are legit. They need to be validated in some way. We need to know what separates them from everyone else who wants us to follow them, listen to them, and adopt their plan or vision.

> Now as Jesus passed by, He saw a man who was blind from birth. And His disciples asked Him, saying, "Rabbi, who sinned, this man or his parents, that he was born blind?" Jesus answered, "Neither this man nor his parents sinned, but that

the works of God should be revealed in him. I must work the works of Him who sent Me while it is day; the night is coming when no one can work."...And He said to him, "Go, wash in the pool of Siloam" (which is translated, Sent). So he went and washed, and came back seeing...."If this Man were not from God, He could do nothing."...Jesus heard that they had cast him out; and when He had found him, He said to him, "Do you believe in the Son of God?" He answered and said, "Who is He, Lord, that I may believe in Him?" And Jesus said to him, "You have both seen Him and it is He who is talking with you." Then he said, "Lord, I believe!" And he worshiped Him.[7]

JESUS DEMONSTRATED AND AUTHENTICATED WHO HE WAS

To see someone turn tasteless water into fine wine was impressive. But Jesus did even more than that. He demonstrated that He was the Son of God through the impressions He made on people. He helped form accurate perceptions in people. The way Jesus loved the people who were with Him demonstrated that He was more than just another strong teacher or good person.

Jesus took it a step further and consistently authenticated all of His actions with the power of God that was displayed in and through Him. Think about it; you see someone love the people who ridicule them...that gets your attention. You see someone tell a lame man to get his mat and get out of dodge. You *know* something is up. You begin to really believe that the guy is who He says He is. Jesus demonstrated and authenticated who He was and who His Father was through Him.

> When Jesus heard that, He said, "This sickness is not unto death, but for the glory of God, that the Son of God may be glorified through it."...Then they took away the stone from the place where the dead man was lying. And Jesus lifted up His eyes and said, "Father, I thank You that You have heard Me. And I know that You always hear Me, but because of the people who are standing by I said this, that they may believe that You sent Me." Now when He had said these things, He cried with a loud voice, "Lazarus, come forth!"...Then many

of the Jews who had come to Mary, and had seen the things Jesus did, believed in Him. But some of them went away to the Pharisees and told them the things Jesus did.[8]

Whatever city you enter, and they receive you, eat such things as are set before you. And heal the sick there, and say to them, "The kingdom of God has come near to you." But whatever city you enter, and they do not receive you, go out into its streets and say, "The very dust of your city which clings to us we wipe off against you. Nevertheless know this, that the kingdom of God has come near you."[9]

Now when He was in Jerusalem at the Passover, during the feast, many believed in His name when they saw the signs which He did.[10]

And truly Jesus did many other signs in the presence of His disciples, which are not written in this book; but these are written that you may believe that Jesus is the Christ, the Son of God, and that believing you may have life in His name.[11]

But if I do, though you do not believe Me, believe the works, that you may know and believe that the Father is in Me, and I in Him.[12]

You see, being "a good person" wasn't enough for even the Son of God. Jesus took it a step further and made people believe in Him because of what He did. Jesus had a positive impact on the people He met because of who He was and what He did. This made Him legit in the eyes of those who watched—and made Him craveable.

The power of God makes Jesus craveable to others.

How can I demonstrate the power of God to others?

20

I DEMONSTRATE THE POWER OF GOD

When we brought you the Good News, it was not only with words but also with power...[1]

 If you aren't showing power, it isn't the gospel.

I CAN'T TELL YOU about it. You will have to just see it for yourself." Have you ever told someone that? Words alone simply can't do justice to some things. You can't tell someone how beautiful a painting is, the majesty of a snow-covered mountain peak, or how life altering it is to witness the birth of your own child.

Most things that bring lasting change come by way of experience. What you see firsthand is something no one can take away from you. When our personal mission is to introduce others to an incredible life with Jesus, our words alone are not enough. The power of Jesus must be demonstrated and experienced. I have to follow the example of Jesus to employ the best way to impact people. The way Jesus did it worked!

+ Demonstrate whom they should believe

+ Communicate whom they need to know

+ Imitate who they need to be

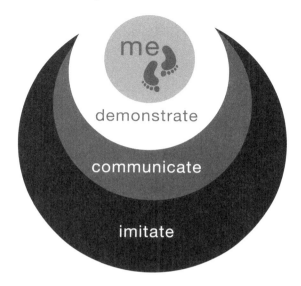

What attracts others to us is the power of God demonstrated through us. That's what attracted people to Jesus, and so it should be with us. Our morality, Bible knowledge, or acts of kindness are by-products of our love for God, not our drawing cards for others.

> Our lives, through abiding in Christ and the Spirit's power, are an invitation to those not yet in the ecclesia, to join us as they see us bringing God's kingdom into our sphere of influence.[2]

If you want to impact people, let God demonstrate His power though you. Completely surrender yourself for His purposes. Your righteousness is not that impressive. Unbelievers can be as righteous as—and some are more righteous than—you are. That does not prove anything. Honestly, you're not that great. But the God who lives in you—He rocks, and He draws people to Himself when He is lifted up. Give people the power of God, not spam!

Our morality can be admired at times from those who are far from God. But in the rare cases that our morality is admired, it can also be a discouragement because people believe they can't live up to God's standards. Our lives offer no hope for them. They misinterpret our moral standards as works that God requires that crowds out space for what we really need—God's grace.

> If I do not do the works of My Father, do not believe Me; but
> if I do, though you do not believe Me, believe the works, that
> you may know and believe that the Father is in Me, and I in
> Him.[3]

A few years ago I started to write down how many different jobs
I've had. I counted thirty-two of them. Can you beat that? One of
the jobs I disliked the most was a job selling business copiers. I had
to load up the copier in my van and make door-to-door cold calls. I
felt like a vacuum cleaner salesman. Not that there's anything wrong
with that, but I think that might be the hardest job ever created.

My strategy was to hand out brochures about the copier I was
trying to sell. This was back when the digital color copier was first
being introduced to the market. It was a great machine. I would
go into an office and show them my brochures and try to convince
them to buy one of these new digital marvels. Do you know that I
never sold one copier like that?

My employer understood the value of demonstrating to a potential buyer how the digital copying machine worked, and in order for
me to be reimbursed for my travel expenses, I had to have a certain
number of what they called "demos" per month. The boss knew that
my standing in someone's office and showing them a piece of paper
was not going to make them want to buy the copier in the back of
my van. What needed to happen was for me to take the copier out
and demonstrate how it actually worked. Once I took that bad boy
in and they saw what it could do, that's when they would consider
buying it. I had to take it out and allow them to see it.

This is what I knew I had to do to sell copiers successfully: demonstrate before I communicate!

The same is true about the kingdom of God. I have to let them
see the kingdom before I *tell* them kingdom things. We are made in
the image of God and called to reflect the image of His Son, Jesus.
Whether they recognize it or not, all of God's created beings are
eagerly waiting for the sons of God to be revealed. If you're a son of
God, you have an obligation to make that reflection craveable!

Show them *who* God is before you tell them *what* God said.

I love the story in Acts when Peter and his crew were thrown in prison for declaring the gospel. Remember, they were thrown in there by the "religious folk," not those they were trying to impact.

Well, they were all in prison singing and talking about Jesus, but not one of the guards overhearing all this showed any interest in joining their little imprisoned crew. That was about to change though. When an angel came and shook the prison and all the doors were thrown open, a guard who was about to commit suicide fell on the ground and asked, "Sirs, what must I do to be saved?"[4] That's what I'm talking about! Believing God to *show* who He is before we begin to *tell* who He is opens people's hearts to the gospel. The original show and tell is demonstrated in the Bible!

You need to show somebody something that's really fantastic before you try to talk with them about it. We must demonstrate before we communicate. What we demonstrate authenticates what we are about to communicate.

What we have been taught is to present the gospel in a way that actually offends those who have no understanding of it. Let me give you an example. A billboard was put up in my town recently. To the right there was a picture of Jesus with thorns on His head and blood running down His face. The middle of the billboard read in bold letters, "Depart, I never knew you."

Now imagine I'm driving down the road in a desperate situation. I see this billboard, and I'm certain this is not the answer to my problems. Why would I look to Jesus if He is only going to tell me that He didn't know me? Christian people, you are not talking to one another when you present the gospel in this way. You are talking to people out of bounds. They do not understand insider language. People out of bounds and looking for answers are *not* getting your message. Demonstrate the message first. You are only trying to communicate, and that communication is sad, at best. We do the kingdom of God a tremendous disservice by trying to talk to people before we demonstrate to people.

> The kingdom of God is not in word but in power.[5]

Paul said, "For the creation eagerly waits with anticipation for God's sons to be revealed."[6] God creates us. No matter what someone tells you or what you've heard, there's not a person in the world who doesn't have an innate desire deep inside to reconnect with their Creator.

All the major religions of the world have writings and teachings of wisdom, morality, and leadership. So if we approach someone with the basic idea that Jesus is the only way to live a "good life," we are overstating our case. Why should they believe us? What are we doing to draw a line of distinction from the kingdom to all the other "isms" out there?

So how do they know that it isn't Muhammad or Buddha, or if two buzzards bumped butts and I popped out. Scripture says that all of creation is crying out to God, "Will You *please* reveal Yourself?" They must see the God of the universe in us. Then they will say, like the jailer, "I want what you got. I know I'm out clubbing on Fridays and I look like I'm having a good time, but I'm really dying on the inside. I'm not going to change my morality to live like you, but if you can tell me that I can have a relationship with my Creator, the living God, and all the power of heaven were to live in me, I want you to tell me about that. But before you can tell me, I got to know you are the real deal. For goodness sake, demonstrate! Show me something!"

> God's life in us expresses itself as *God's* life, not as a human life trying to be godly.[7]

Paul wrote the Corinthians, "And I, brethren, when I came to you, did not come with excellence of speech or of wisdom declaring to you the testimony of God."[8] Paul had a call from God; he understood the mission.

"Paul, go out and help people find, follow, and be like Jesus."

"Yes, Lord. I am there."

"You have to go out and bring in those who are out of bounds."

"Who are they?"

"It's the Gentiles, Paul. Go to the Gentiles"

"Yes, Lord."

"Go to Corinth."

"Yes, Lord."

And when he shows up, he did come and explain all the testimony of God.

The next part says, "I was with you. I was just with you." Do you understand? Paul was a Pharisee. He was one of the most educated people of his day. He knew all the answers, but when he first showed up, he did not try to give them all the answers. When he first had an encounter with them, he was just with them. Is that simple enough for you?

So many times we just want to jump over that step and want to tell people so much without just being with them. I don't have answers to all the questions, but I can tell you what God is challenging me to do. Every single day God calls us to be on mission. That means every single day I am to help people find, follow and be like Jesus. And the way that I do that is to bring those in who are out of bounds. And I ask God, "God, who is it out of bounds that You want my life to impact?" Then the first thing they need to see in me is the power of God.

What does the power of God look like in my life? Quite honestly, I'm not real sure what that looks like. But when I read Scripture and look at the life of Jesus, I see His example. Every single time Jesus went to a new place or new town, He performed some kind of miracle. And when He did, people gathered to hear what He had to say. And Jesus said the things that we saw Him do, we would do greater things. And I still don't know exactly what all that means.

My wife, Georgie, was born and raised in Liberia, West Africa. We both love that country and its people. We visit there often and are involved in several ministries in the country. Recently we were spending time with a group of pastors who were helping to plant churches in the cities and rural areas.

After one of our meetings one of the pastors told me a story. He said recently he was talking to a man and telling him he should serve Jesus. The man asked him, "Why should I serve Jesus? Look at you. You live in a mud house, and I live in a blockhouse. You have worn out clothes; I have nice clothes. Your children are not in school; my children are in school and eat rice every night while your children go to bed hungry. Why should I serve Jesus? It seems to me you should be serving my god."

The pastor then looked at me and asked, "What should I tell him, Daddy?" (In Liberia they call their spiritual leaders "daddy.") Maybe

I should have told this sincere pastor, "Oh, yeah, well, your reward is in heaven; you will have a great big house there and all the rice you can eat." But I was not sure what to tell him. I know questions like these happen in other places, including America. The "perfect" answer is not the point of my story. My point is that Christians often live powerless lives that are not craveable at all to unbelievers. I am not preaching a prosperity gospel. No way. But I do believe people who follow Jesus should live blessed and craveable lives. Jesus seems to make no difference in the way that most Christ-followers live. I believe God planned much more for us in this life as well as the next—not for our benefit alone, but to make Him famous.

I know the way we are doing it now is not working. One reason is because we are relying on people being attracted to our morality. Our morality is not a demonstration of God's power. I've never seen anyone come into the kingdom of God because they were attracted to someone's morality. So what I would challenge you to do is what God is challenging me to do. And that's simply one word: surrender. God's word is clear:

> Because the Good News we brought to you came not only with words, but with power, with the Holy Spirit, and with sure knowledge that it is true. Also you know how we lived when we were with you in order to help you.[9]

If you persuade someone with just words, someone who comes after you may have more persuasive words than you. The issue is both words and power. And the God of the universe wants to demonstrate His power through you!

▨▶ I show God before I tell what God says.

◊ Where do I see the power of God most in my life?

HE COMMUNICATED THE PURPOSE OF GOD

Do you not believe that I am in the Father, and the Father in Me? The words that I speak to you I do not speak on My own authority; but the Father who dwells in Me does the works.[1]

 Jesus's plan was for me to be like Him.

ON'T BE AFRAID. I will catch you, son." These words are difficult to believe when you are about to make your maiden leap into the deep end of the pool! At least my son struggled to believe. When we see something scary, our first inclination is to draw back in fear. But hearing and trusting the person who is telling you to jump can give just enough courage to leap.

Life is difficult, and Jesus knew it. He was living it out day by day. When those around Him came to know Him, He began to explain to them, "If you abide in my word, you are truly my disciples, and you will know the truth, and the truth will set you free."[2]

Once Jesus demonstrated whom they should believe, He then began to teach them whom they needed to know. The real purpose for which they were created was to know the Father. Jesus equipped and encouraged those who followed Him with what they needed to successfully navigate life as His true followers.

> Now it is God who has made us for this very purpose and has given us the Spirit as a deposit, guaranteeing what is to come.[3]

The truth is, as new believers in Jesus, the purpose of God was for them to become like Jesus.

> And we, who with unveiled faces all reflect the Lord's glory, are being transformed into his likeness with ever-increasing glory, which comes from the Lord, who is the Spirit.[4]

So Jesus communicated and taught what being like Him would look like.

> These words you hear are not my own; they belong to the Father who sent me.[5]

This was so different from what people had heard from their religious leaders. Those leaders were more concerned that others become pious and self-righteous like them. Then Jesus comes along and changes everything. He said, "Take my yoke upon you. Let me teach you, because I am humble and gentle at heart, and you will find rest for your souls."[6] The burdens the Pharisees were putting on the people were unbearable and unattainable! Jesus was offering rest. What is your preference? Sounds like a no-brainer to me.

Many had made it seem like a life walking in the purpose of God was some high wall of righteousness that was impossible to conquer. But God's plan and purpose are simple: just be like Jesus. But that is simpler to understand than do. Yet anything of great value comes at a great price.

Don't lose sight of the simplicity of God's purpose. If we complicate it, we will be doing what the Pharisees did and changing the plan of God in order to make ourselves look better.

The purpose of God, us becoming like Jesus, is a day-by-day process.

> Therefore we do not lose heart. Even though our outward man is perishing, yet the inward man is being renewed day by day.[7]

Every day is a new day. We can't stay where we were yesterday. We look to God every day to be made new and transformed into the image of Christ.

This day-by-day purpose goes back to some of the things we've already covered and saw modeled by Jesus.

- ✦ We look to God's Word.

- ✦ We listen to God's voice.

- ✦ We live out God's mission.

This purpose of being like Jesus is hard-core, especially when we have to do life at the same time that we are being like Jesus. It would be easier if we could just set aside a quiet time and place and say, "OK, for the next thirty minutes I'm going to be like Jesus." Well, that's not reality. Being like Jesus in the midst of difficulty is fulfilling the purpose of God. But we have His promise to help us be what we could not be without Him.

> For our light and momentary troubles are achieving for us an eternal glory that far outweighs them all. So we fix our eyes not on what is seen, but on what is unseen. For what is seen is temporary, but what is unseen is eternal.[8]

> It is the Spirit who gives life; the flesh profits nothing. The words that I speak to you are spirit, and they are life.[9]

> The Lord will fulfill [his purpose] for me; your love, O Lord, endures forever.[10]

> Indeed I have spoken it; I will also bring it to pass. I have purposed it; I will also do it.[11]

One of the things Jesus communicated best about the Father was about the life God wants people in His kingdom to have. God isn't about killing people because of their sin, but rather He is giving life. Jesus communicated the heart of the Father.

▰▰ My purpose to be like Jesus is a lifelong journey.

🔥 What area in my life am I least/most like Jesus?

22

I COMMUNICATE THE PURPOSE OF GOD

My word and my preaching was not in persuasive words of human wisdom, but in demonstration of the Spirit and of power—that your faith may not be in the wisdom of men, but in the power of God.[1]

⬤ When I speak of kingdom things, people should be ready to hear.

A WHILE BACK I was invited to go play golf with some friends. I was out on the putting green, and this guy came up to me trying to give me pointers on my putting technique. All I could hear was…"blah, blah, blah." I thought to myself about how I was going to impress him with my skills once we got out on the course. Well, we got out there, and it turns out that this guy was a professional golfer. He was incredible and just showing me up! (So much for my man pride.) He was tearing up the course the entire time!

Toward the end of the game I casually walked up close to him and said, "Now what were you trying to tell me earlier?" Yeah! I want to hear want you have to say now. When I see you know what you're talking about proven by how you "play," everything changes. When I see evidence that you really have something to tell me, your advice becomes important.

Remember this…

We demonstrate before we communicate. The golf pro

demonstrated to me that he certainly had something of value to communicate to me. So…I listened.

As authentic followers of Jesus we are in the process of fulfilling the purpose of God by becoming like Jesus. This means we communicate the purpose of God to others. And there are two groups we need to communicate that purpose to: those outside the kingdom and those inside the kingdom.

THOSE OUTSIDE THE KINGDOM

This is generally a scary thing, talking about "God and kingdom stuff" with someone not in the kingdom yet. Kingdom talk can sound a little cultic, you know. You can come across like, "Me, my peeps, and Jesus are going to take over the world, so you better get on our side before the revolution." You can't come across to unbelievers as someone who is looking to prove to the world that you are right and everyone else is stupid.

Jesus invites people into relationship with Him and promptly revolutionizes their lives when they accept the invite. The political and theological view of a "Rambo Jesus" does not fit. Unfortunately our mind-sets can be similar to some of Jesus's followers in Bible times. They wanted Jesus to take over *now*. Everything that was making their lives miserable would be fixed when Jesus took over…they hoped.

Even after Jesus's resurrection His followers were still looking for the quick fix. He had taught them for forty days about "the kingdom of God." And even the post-resurrection Jesus had to feel frustrated when they missed an essential part of the lesson.

Think about it for a minute. Jesus Christ, the Son of God, personally leads you through a forty-day kingdom seminar—not by video, not one of His associates, but He is leading live! And you miss part of the point. The participants asked, "Lord, will You at this time restore the kingdom to Israel?"[2] First of all, wrong kingdom. Second of all, no! Do I believe one day Jesus will reign over the world forever? Absolutely! The Bible makes it clear.[3] But not now, not yet.

However, if we understand that God is working in the other person, preparing him to hear the words that the Spirit leads you to share, then mentioning the kingdom could be an important perspective. Following Jesus is much more significant than an offer of temporary relief from life's difficulties.

Jesus's kingdom is big and eternal.

> At the name of Jesus every knee should bow, in heaven and on earth and under the earth, and every tongue confess that Jesus Christ is Lord, to the glory of God the Father.[4]

The kingdom is great truth to tell if we are operating in conjunction with God and not just saying something because we think we must. Jesus is not one "spiritual path" among many. He is Lord!

Jesus said not to be afraid of what you will say. The Spirit will give you the words. But if you are at a place where the Spirit didn't lead you, He's not going to lead you as to what to say. Communicating kingdom truth is to be done at the right time. And when the time is right to communicate kingdom purposes to those outside, you will know it.

THOSE INSIDE THE KINGDOM

We communicate the purpose of God by walking and talking it. You "walkie talkie." You know what a walkie-talkie is, right? The walkie-talkie is a communication device developed by the US military in the 1950s. The innovation allowed commanders to walk and talk at the same time without being tied down to one location. But the "walk" came before the "talk."

Our actions and words are inseparable in the minds of others. They both communicate together, and if one contradicts the other, one can cancel the effectiveness of the other.

> A large portion of the lost world looks at the Church as a pathetic entity made up of a bunch of nincompoops who aren't serious about what they do or say.[5]

Not long ago I had an unannounced visitor come to the church office. Normally I only have time for scheduled appointments, but I saw this visitor because something caught my attention. His card read, "Detective 'So and So' from the Narcotics Division of the Sheriff's Department." See, the name on that little card demonstrated some power that I needed to pay attention to. You understand what I'm saying. It authenticated what he was about to communicate to me. He had my undivided attention as he spoke!

Our lives (what we do and say) communicate volumes. So what we do needs to match what we say. When we communicate God's purposes to others, they should see our lives as living examples of what we are talking about. And they should hear us talk, teach, and preach those same God-inspired purposes laid out in Scripture.

> The Father who sent Me gave Me a command, what I should say and what I should speak.[6]

> Let your conversation be gracious and attractive so that you will have the right response for everyone.[7]

So it was with Jesus. His power demonstrated to the Samaritan woman that she needed to hear what He had to say. And so He began to share with her about the heavenly Father and impart some spiritual truths to her. The woman said she knew the Messiah was coming and that He would speak all truth. He told her, "I who speak to you am He."[8]

Oh, wow, all of a sudden you see what has occurred in the process. Jesus shows up on a mission, and here is a woman who is not just out of bounds but way out of bounds.

And Jesus begins to demonstrate His power, which authenticated what He was about to communicate. Watch what happened after the woman's encounter with Jesus. She went back to her city, and "she told the people, 'Come see a man who knew all about the things I did, who knows me inside and out. Do you think this could be the Messiah?' And they went out to see for themselves."[9] She was in awe, and other people in her city knew it. They listened to her when she asked them to "come see a man..." Jesus gave her craveability that she had never known for His mission. So the people went to the well. They went looking. They went to see with their own eyes. People want to see the power of God before they hear about God.

And many of the Samaritans believed in Him because of the woman who testified. Take note that her influence had nothing to do with her morality. She was living with a man she wasn't married to and had been previously married five times. How about that for a moral résumé? But they believed because of her authentic encounter with God.

Too often we just want to go around and tell people what the Bible says. How many of you came to understand the kingdom because of that? Not me! I came into the kingdom because someone took the time to formulate a relationship with me. One of the ways we can demonstrate God's power is through stories, God's stories.

The woman at the well was able to demonstrate God's power because of her God story. Many of you don't have any God stories. Something is wrong with this picture. We should always have God stories to share. If we are really living with the power of the Holy Spirit, we should have stories to tell about His miraculous power. I'm not talking about what God did in your life twenty years ago. I'm talking about what He did last week, this week, and today.

Once someone is ready to hear what we have to say, we know we aren't wasting our words or "[casting] our pearls before swine."[10] That saying was not meant to be harsh. It is an unforgettable picture to teach us that we can have something of great value, but if the person we are giving it to doesn't understand its value, it will be wasted.

Most of the time Christians want to go straight to what God has said and tell someone that the Bible says, "Don't do this, or you must do that." Certainly the person hearing someone communicate what God has said, without knowing if the person is authentic, will quickly dismiss the info.

If kingdom power is not evident in my life, people will not listen to my words.

What could be stopping God's power in my life?

23

HE IMITATED THE PERSON OF GOD

If I do not do the works of my Father, do not believe Me.[1]

⬤ Jesus put real flesh on who the Father was.

I WAS VERY PRIVILEGED to have spent time with a man who showed me the heart of God. My father-in-law, Henry Irby Hungerpiller, was the grandson of German immigrants to the United States. In the middle of a wild street meeting in downtown Singapore during World War II, he gave his all to Jesus, and he did give it all.

He served Jesus's kingdom in the West African country of Liberia (the birthplace of my wife) for nearly thirty-five years. "Dad and Mom" were still in Liberia for fifteen years after Georgie and I were married. I made many trips to Liberia while Dad was still there. I went everywhere from the beach to the bush with him. I watched closely as he showed the heart of God to all those he met.

His impact on my life is immeasurable. I would not, and could not, be doing what I'm doing now if I had not seen the heart of God imitated before my very eyes in the life of one of His most humble servants. He helped me become the "God-me."

Just as the most craveable thing we can be is a reflection of Jesus, the most craveable thing Jesus could be was a reflection of the Father.

To see me is to see the Father.[2]

He was saying, "I am a perfect reflection; I have perfectly imitated who and what My Father is."

Once when the "religious leaders" were really questioning Jesus as to who He was, He got tired of the badgering and said, "Before Abraham was, I am."[3] What? Those guys wanted to go spider monkey on Jesus and tear Him from limb to limb, but He escaped. They didn't like that He was saying He and the Great I Am were the same.

> Imitate—*to copy, mimic, or try to be like*

Jesus really put "flesh" on the heart and person of the Father. From the beginning of time God would reveal Himself to only a few. But for the most part the very person and heart of God was somewhat of a mystery, until Jesus. It's no wonder that when Jesus came and said, "If you have seen me, you have seen the Father," they wanted to stone Him! How could He say such a thing. Nobody has ever seen God!

That was right, but Jesus said, "The Father and I are one. We are the same in every way. So watch Me, listen to Me, follow Me, and see My heart, and You will understand who God, Yahweh, the Great I Am really is!"

As His followers lived and walked with Jesus every day, they were able to see and understand the heart of the Father, because Jesus imitated, demonstrated, and put it on display for all to see. And when we are able to not just hear what should be done but see it first, its impact and understanding are multiplied exponentially.

Remember the prayer of Jesus in John 17? Jesus prayed that the people who followed Him for the rest of eternity would be one just as He and the Father were one. Jesus was one with the Father. Jesus imitated the Father in every area of His life. From Jesus's talk to His miracles to the way He loved unconditionally, Jesus was one with the Father.

> You must have the same attitude that Christ Jesus had.[4]

▨ Jesus showed how to measure if
your heart is like God's heart.

🔥 What part of my heart looks the most like God's heart?

24

I IMITATE THE PERSON OF GOD

Love your enemies, bless those who curse you, do good to those who hate you, and pray for those who spitefully use you and persecute you, that you may be sons of your Father in heaven.[1]

● People who look at me should say, "I'll
bet that is what Jesus is like."

I REMEMBER WHEN I returned to finish college after having a family. We had no "real income" for three years. I did odd jobs when I could. Georgie was home with our first daughter. She generated income from home and was quite the entrepreneur. But all our efforts to make ends meet fell short more often than not.

On one occasion that shortfall was quite a drop. I received some news that hurt my "man pride" like nothing else could. My wife told me that she and my daughter Rebecca were hungry, they had eaten the last bit of pancake mix, and there was literally nothing left to eat.

All I could do was go into panic mode (and prayer mode for those who want to "Jesus juke" me). I remembered an ad in the newspaper offering twenty dollars for a blood plasma donation. I thought, "How hard or painful can that be?" I got the address and stood in line for an hour behind all those who seemed to frequent this "easy money" spot.

Well, it finally became my turn. I was strapped in, held down, and drained of all (what seemed like) my blood, plasma, bodily fluids, and strength! Then I was injected with some milky cold Freon-feeling material that I was sure was embalming fluid! Finally

I was unstrapped after the three-hour drain and refill. I was given my twenty dollars and asked to come back. NOT! I was so not going back.

I bought some chicken and bread for my family with the twenty dollars. When I brought it home, they were glad to have it, and I was happy to have the hardest earned twenty-spot ever. "A man's gotta do what a man's gotta do!"

Jesus did what He had to do. Jesus personified "a man's gotta do what a man's gotta do." He did what had to be done, and we are required to do the same. As Jesus reflected the image of His Father, we are to imitate the Father as well.

In Matthew 5 Jesus gives a great checklist of the heart of the Father with some practical application to see how well we are imitating God to others:

> You have heard that it was said, "You shall love your neighbor and hate your enemy." But I say to you, love your enemies, bless those who curse you, do good to those who hate you, and pray for those who spitefully use you and persecute you, that you may be sons of your Father in heaven; for He makes His sun rise on the evil and on the good, and sends rain on the just and on the unjust. For if you love those who love you, what reward have you? Do not even the tax collectors do the same? And if you greet your brethren only, what do you do more than others? Do not even the tax collectors do so? Therefore you shall be perfect, just as your Father in heaven is perfect.[2]

Show love, even to those who hate me

"But I say to you, love your enemies." That's a tall order. Only through the power of the Spirit working in us are we able to demonstrate such a commitment. God demonstrated His love for us while we were still His enemies.[3]

Bless (say good things about, and wish well) those who curse (say something to intentionally hurt) me

"Bless those who curse you." Now this goes against everything that is in me! When someone comes at me and says untrue, hurtful, or spiteful things, I want to go at them with more than my words! I'm looking for a way to bring them pain.

But when Jesus was accused, He didn't answer any false accusation brought against Him. He remained silent. I have learned this. If I defend myself, that's all I get. However, if I let God take up for me, His revenge is better than mine ever could have been! I'm not saying we wish ill on anyone, but God doesn't take it lightly when someone speaks evil of another of His servants.

Do good to those who hate me!

Come on, it's hard enough to keep my mouth closed, but I have to open my hand and actually *do* something good for somebody who can't stand me! That has to be a God-attitude right there. But straight up honest, there will be those outside and inside the kingdom who will just not like you.

I was shopping at the grocery store one day, and I saw a lady who has hated me for years! She is supposed to be a believer, but she just can't stand me and she doesn't care that others know it. Well, it had been more than five years since I had seen her. When she saw me coming through the fresh produce, she quickly gave the "I am appalled at you" head turn and ran through the fresh fruit looking for a quick getaway!

I took off in hot pursuit. I stalked her through the frozen pizza aisle and waited in ambush. I peered through the Cheetos display as she came up toward the front. Then I pulled in front of her where she could not avoid eye contact. I said, "Hi! How are you?" There was a short grunting sound, followed by another disgusted head turn. I failed. I should have offered to carry her groceries to the car!

Pray for those who spitefully use and persecute me

Honestly, praying for those I love and really care about is difficult enough, but actually praying for those who are spiteful and relentlessly put me down—oh my! That reminds me of the country song "I Pray for You" by Joel Brentlinger and Jaron Lowenstein. He explains in the song that he was hurt by a woman and went to church and asked the preacher what he should do. The preacher told him he can't hold anything against anyone who hurts him. The only thing he could do was pray for her. The guy must not have understood, because he began to pray for her all kinds of disasters to come into her life. Now that is not the kind of praying Jesus was talking about.

We need to have genuine caring even for those who cause us great pain and hurt. I gave plasma because I knew that's what I had to do in spite of the pain. In the same way we are called to be like God no matter how difficult or painful it may be.

> Therefore you shall be perfect, just as your Father in heaven is perfect.[4]

When I'm with other believers, they should see that I imitate Jesus. They should see my Father in me. I have to be *craveable* to those outside and in the kingdom. I can't help someone be like Jesus if I'm not imitating Jesus. They won't know what that looks like.

This is a huge part of our mission. This takes being transparent, open, and honest. We have to let people close enough to see what drives us and who we really are at the core.

CRAVEABLE MAKEOVER

My secret desire when I was in high school was to be the person everybody wanted to be around. As hard as I tried, I never could get there. Hopefully I have made a case that you should have similar desires but for a much higher purpose. You should want to be the kind of person that lost people want to be around. Look at Jesus's example: "By this time a lot of men and women of doubtful reputation were hanging around Jesus, listening intently."[5] Jesus didn't have to hang around people of "doubtful reputation." They wanted to hang around Him!

Deep in our hearts as believers God will make us hungry for lost friends. But either because we are afraid or just plain uncomfortable, we may avoid taking steps to do that. We all crave the affections and adoration of others. We also want acceptance and approval from our peers. However, few ever fully understand the real things that make us attractive to others. This is absolutely vital as we seek to gain influence in the lives of those around us for the kingdom of God. Below I have listed five habits that will actually help people crave to be with you.

1. Listen to others' ideas. Nobody likes a know-it-all. So get over your own ideas and actually become interested in someone else's ideas. We all like to talk about ourselves and what we think. So when we find a person who cares what we think—*bam!*—we love to be with them! By listening, Jesus made others feel loved and important. Through listening, Jesus gave a gift to people that few others ever gave. This made Him attractive to be around.

2. Speak only good things about others. Let me tell you a little secret. If you think talking about others (gossiping) is going to win you juicy friends, you are in for a world of hurt! If you talk negatively about someone else around someone, they are going to ask themselves, "What are they saying about me?" Gossip will ruin your reputation and sabotage trust in a friendship. Don't go there!

3. Give generously when you can. Nobody likes a mooch. Don't develop a reputation as the "cheap-o" of the group. Proverbs says, "Everyone is the friend of a person who gives gifts!"[6] Generosity makes people feel valued and not used! So always pick up one or two more dinner checks. Bring something to dinner—your billfold! Be the one everyone knows will be generous. Being generous is not an issue of amount but rather attitude! Remember the widow's mite.

4. Initiate with others. If you are sitting by the phone waiting for the invitation, you are in for a long wait! Get over yourself and make the contact. I know it is hard, always feeling you have to make the first move, but that's just the way it is. People feel appreciated and valued when we make the first move, but don't keep score! Just always make the move. Done!

5. Authenticity is irreplaceable! Don't try to be several different people around different groups. You will

always be found out! Too many people will do anything to fit into their surroundings to be accepted.
Like chameleons, they change colors quickly. But the
best way to help people is to be the same color all the
time. Be real! Don't be a chameleon—be yourself!
Trust who God made you to be—that will make you
truly craveable.[7]

These are some things I have noticed that make me attracted to
others and even makes them craveable! Any others you have noticed?

There are many more attitudes and behaviors God will plant in
your life if you really want to be craveable. But you have to start
somewhere. Stop now. Review the list above and ask God where you
need to start this week. What step will you take to become more
craveable?

I am to "walk as Jesus walked." When people see me, they should
see a craveable reflection of Jesus.

━━━

**▞▶ Showing power, talking kingdom, and
loving others will show Jesus.**

━━━

〰〰〰〰〰〰〰〰〰〰〰〰〰〰〰〰〰〰〰〰〰〰〰〰〰

🔥 How can I show Jesus to others this week?

〰〰〰〰〰〰〰〰〰〰〰〰〰〰〰〰〰〰〰〰〰〰〰〰〰

PART 6

CRAVEABLE LEARNING

He who rejects change is the architect of decay.[1]

LEARNING NEW THINGS is always a challenge, frankly because learning something new means changing how we are doing something now. Most of us really push back from learning and changing. Once we learn how to get something done and feel some level of mastery, we become very complacent.

I think that attitude is seen a lot with technology. How many people do you know who fought getting a cell phone? Said they would never have a computer in their home, never wanted Internet service, and didn't see the value of a portable tablet or smartphone? The fact is, there are many things we have to get done, but how we can do them or how we should do them is constantly changing.

Think of it like this. If you owned a business and wanted to stay in business, you know *what* you have to do: get customers to buy your product or service. You also know *what must be done*: collect payment for your product of service. Now *how* you've accomplished those two things in your business over the last twenty years has changed tremendously.

We always need to be learning new ways to get done what we have to accomplish; if not, we become obsolete and get so far behind we lose any prospect of attracting new customers.

25

HE KNEW HOW TO
GET THINGS DONE

Who needs a doctor: the healthy or the sick?
I'm here inviting the sin-sick...[1]

⬤ Jesus knew the "what"; the Father told Him how.

I HAVE A GOOD friend who's a doctor. I was really sick once and went to see him. And as a good doctor should, he asked me a ton of questions! He ran all kinds of tests and entered them into a database he was able to access on his smartphone. He was able to make some recommendations for treatment based on all the data he collected.

What really struck me about that experience was the fact that we are all different. No matter what, when we are sick and go to the doctor, our age, overall health, past sicknesses, and other issues make each person unique and in need of an individualized treatment plan.

Jesus sure understood that. He said He came to bring healing to the sick, and let me tell you, we are all sick in some way. But the principle is still the same: how He "treated" each person was different, no two alike. Jesus knew what needed to be done, but He had to depend on the Father to tell Him how to treat each person so they would respond to the offer of real life.

Jesus looked to the Father to tell Him how to do what He told Him to do and what must be done. Every day of Jesus's life was filled with opportunities. As He journeyed on His mission, there were many situations where He needed the Father to tell Him how to get the mission done.

At every new place Jesus stepped into, there were challenges to face, decisions to be made, and obstacles to overcome. Every new step and every new place generates three questions:

1. What do I do here?

2. What has to get done here?

3. How do I get it done?

You see, Jesus knew that what He had to do and get done wasn't enough. He had to know how to do it. How something is done has endless possibilities, but only one with God-ability comes from God. The Father had a "how" for every place Jesus went.

- How do I heal this guy? "Spit on the ground, make mud, and put it on his eyes."

- How do I heal this guy? "Take his hand and make him walk."

- How do I heal this guy? "Don't even go to his house; just speak and it will be done."

Remember, Jesus said He only did and said what the Father said! Jesus was always listening for the right "how." God never changes in character, but how He does things changes constantly.

> As for God, His way is perfect; the word of the LORD is proven.[2]

> As you do not know the path of the wind, or how the body is formed in a mother's womb, so you cannot understand the work of God.[3]

> Then Jesus answered and said to them, "Most assuredly, I say to you, the Son can do nothing of Himself, but what He sees the Father do; for whatever He does, the Son also does in like manner. For the Father loves the Son, and shows Him all things that He Himself does; and He will show Him greater works than these, that you may marvel."[4]

We need to understand there's a difference between the "what" and the "how."

God's "what" never changes, but
His "how" is constantly changing.

Who can help me learn God's "how" in
an area I want to serve Him?

26

I KNOW HOW TO GET
THINGS DONE

*I will be with you as you speak, and I will
instruct you in what to say.*[1]

◉ My mission for God never changes,
but the "how" is always changing.

REMEMBER ONE OF the worst of my more than thirty jobs,
selling copiers? I had to go around and demonstrate copying
machines to businesses—kind of like a door-to-door
salesman.

So my sales manager told me what I must do: I must demonstrate these machines to businesses. But he also told me what must be done: "Artie, you must sell thirty thousand dollars in machines every month!" I really had to demonstrate how craveable those copiers were to sell that many. Wow, that was pretty heavy. There were six to eight other salespeople in our office, and we all had the same two "whats":

1. What must I do? Demonstrate the value and power
   of the copier.

2. What must be done? Sell copiers.

But we were all different. Some of us had to sell to certain towns and cities; others were specialists in medical, education, and industry.

No two of us were the same. But we were all given the same "what you must do" and "what must be done."

The sales manager sat down with each of us and told us individually how to sell to the customer base we were responsible for. Since each customer base was different, it required a different "how." You can't make a copier craveable to a school principal by demonstrating how it can accomplish medical applications. Each of us had to learn our own "how" because each of us was different and had different customers to reach.

At each step of life, every time we move into a new chapter or season of life, we need to ask those two questions:

1. "What must I do" here in this place?

2. "How" do I do it?

In our journey on the field of the kingdom, we will have many steps and many places to stand and ask God how.

"How?" is by far the biggest question I'm asked all the time. As a pastor, leader, or coach, I am asked by everyone how to do something. With marriage, kids, money, relationships, staff, or church, the "how" question is the biggest.

Most of those asking this question don't realize they are asking the wrong question to the wrong person. Many ask how to get something done and yet not know what they need to do. That's like someone asking, "How do I make money in business?", and when you ask them what kind of business they are in, they say, "I don't know."

You see, "the what" has to be known before "the how." When a dad asks, "How do I raise my son to love God?", I ask him first, "Do you know what you are supposed to do?" In other words, what has God required you to do as a father?

+ Discipline your son.

+ Train you son in the way he should go.

+ Talk about the things of God when you are walking through life with your son.

You see, these are "the whats" that you must do as a father, according to Scripture, to raise a godly son. Now you can't ask how to raise a godly son without knowing what you have to do in order to see that occur.

Now to the how: "How am I to discipline my son?" That is a question you must ask God. I don't know your son, his age, his emotional or physical condition, or his temperament and personality.

It's tempting to use someone else's "how," especially if it's been successful. Let's say a guy is having problems with his wife and feels he's about to lose his marriage. He goes to the bookstore and gets a book on how to be the greatest husband. The book is written by some guy who almost lost his marriage, and he really prayed and sought God about how he could save his marriage.

During his time of seeking God, he reads, "Husbands, love your wives, as Christ loved the church."[2] Immediately God lays on his heart three things:

1. Bring her coffee every morning.

2. Date her once a week.

3. Bring her flowers once a month.

He immediately starts this plan, and it saves his marriage! His wife becomes his biggest fan, and so he decides to write a book and share his secret of how he became the greatest husband and saved his marriage.

Well, this struggling guy says, "That's it. That must be how I can show love to my wife and save my marriage." So he immediately begins to...

1. Bring her coffee every morning

2. Date her once a week

3. Bring her flowers once a month

Well, two years later, she has an affair and leaves him. She kept trying to tell him she didn't like coffee; she liked tea. She wanted a date every night for thirty minutes, not a four-hour date just on

Friday. And she did not want flowers; she liked chocolates. In other words, his wife wasn't feeling the love at all.

So she happened to find a man who loved tea, would talk with her every day for thirty minutes, and bring her chocolates! One size will never fit all in marriage or in ministry. Most of us can figure out the what. But we struggle with the how.

When God reveals the how to us and we begin to walk in that plan and purpose with God, transformation takes place. And that transformation process needs to continue on, day after day, step after step.

My how

This is a life journey. This is a continuous process not a destination. Once you are in the kingdom, it's *your* life in the kingdom. In life we have a lot of steps. We land in different places.

My now-how

We need to be informed. Being informed means we know, understand, and recognize what is being said. Come to God on a daily basis (some of us more than that) and ask Him two questions:

WHAT MUST I DO, AND HOW DO I DO IT?

In every place and with every person God puts in our lives, our mission doesn't change. We impact our friends; we impact our spouses and kids. That's why at every new junction of life comes the question: "What must I do?"

The answer to that question is always found in Scripture. If we don't know what God says we must do, we will certainly be doing the wrong thing!

Too many feel we know what we must do and we keep doing "a how" and feel relieved of the weight of what must be done. We can never fall in love with the how! The moment we fall in love with the how, two things occur.

1. First, we become a Pharisee. We begin to value the process more than the product. We become so focused on how we're going to do this and how we're not going to do that, that we lose sight of our real

end goal. The what isn't going to be perfect. The end goal is to make impact.

2. Second, we stop moving. We stop having to seek God for the how. We stop going into new life seasons with anticipation and excitement because we're comfortable with how we were doing the previous season.

Wherever you are right now, seek God for the how. Just because you knew what you're doing is how you were supposed to do life, ministry, marriage, friendship, or other part of life five years ago, it may not be how you're supposed to do it now.

I can never fall in love with the "how."

What "how" in my life do I need to let go of?

27

I KNOW HOW TO GET THINGS DONE NOW

But you have an anointing from the Holy One, and you know all things.[1]

 Only God's "how" is supernaturally empowered.

COULD YOU SEE a little ten-year-old girl ask her mom, "How do I style my hair, Mom?" Well, the mother shows her how to fix her hair. The mother sees her daughter when she is thirty, and she's doing it the same way! The mother screams "What are you doing? You look like a doofus with your hair like that." The daughter says, "That's how you told me to do it." Mom says, "I told you how to do that twenty years ago. You can't do it that way now!"

It's vital each of us have our own "now how." I can't use another person's how, just like the struggling husband we talked about earlier who tried to use a how from a book by a man who was successful based on his own "now how" and his marriage failed.

It's not just an issue of getting your how; you need to understand that the how changes. It must change. Remember, the how is based on culture and context, and those are constantly shifting and changing. I have been married for almost thirty years. The way I love my wife now is very different than it was twenty, fifteen, or even one year ago! Why? Our context and culture have changed. Age, kids, finances, friends, and emotional stages of life dictate a change in the way I love my wife.

Sometimes finding your "now how" is a matter of creativity—being creative with the limited resources you may have. I'm reminded of one of my father-in-law's stories. While living in Africa for thirty-five years, he had many to tell. In the Liberian culture people know how to use what they have to get things done. They often have to find a "now how" because the original how isn't working.

One day while riding down the road, he noticed a coffin in the back of a pickup truck. There was something strange about this coffin. While the coffin had been made to hold this particular body, the body was not made to hold this particular coffin. Apparently the individual was about two feet taller than the length of the coffin. It's time for the funeral; everything is ready and done; there's no time to make any changes. So the how involved in getting the body into this coffin had to become a "now how" experience.

Well, the solution was creatively simple. The coffin maker knocked out the bottom end of the coffin, which allowed the individual's feet to lay free and flat, although his legs were sticking out of one end of the coffin. Not a problem anymore, at least not in this country. The old how to fit a body in a coffin was not working, so a new how was creatively invented.

Culture does play a role in your "now how." While this solution would not have been acceptable in one culture, it certainly was in another. When we understand how this spiritual principle works, it changes how we see everything. The application touches every part of our lives. Every area of our lives is touched and addressed with a "what we must do" in Scripture. Then we look for the how, and the "now how" God has for us.

As I write this, my wife and I are sitting in a friend's beach house overlooking the water on an early morning, talking and sharing our desires and dreams for the future. My wife asked me how she should measure her progress in something God has called her to accomplish. As I explained how I did that, her response was, "Oh, no, that won't work for me. I need to find how to do that another way." So we researched some tools, and she found one that made her smile so big. "Now this is great. This is just how I need to track my stuff."

Now many of the things that my wife and I have goals to accomplish are the same, but how we are going to do it and how we are going to measure our progress are different.

Think of it this way; the journey of life takes us down a lot of long roads. Some of those roads we need a different car. If we continue to drive the same car, eventually it will break down. However, before a car breaks down, there are generally warning lights that go off.

Unfortunately many of us as individuals, and our circle of friends and churches, are sitting in the middle of the road all crowded in a broken-down ride. We have ignored all the warnings, and we have closed our eyes to the "check engine" light. But since we love that old car, we refuse to abandon it and continue the journey by beginning anew.

You know there's a problem when you are more in love with how you get there than you are in reaching your destination.

> It is written, "Man shall not live by bread alone, but by every word that proceeds from the mouth of God."[2]

> But we all, with unveiled face, beholding as in a mirror the glory of the Lord, are being transformed *into the same image* from glory to glory, just as by the Spirit of the Lord.[3]

Remember, though, with every new step and new place we stand, we must display the kingdom as craveable. Everyone around us is watching us: those on the field with us and those on the sidelines. So we always show the life of a person displaying a craveable King and His incredible kingdom.

The first step is to go to God's Word and ask, "What must I do?" So many want to ask how without knowing what they are supposed to do! It's crazy. I hear the conversations of people, and they are looking desperately to make something succeed, yet they aren't doing the right thing!

> All Scripture is inspired by God and is useful to teach us what is true and to make us realize what is wrong in our lives. It corrects us when we are wrong and teaches us *to do what is right*.[4]

Crop rotation is vital to continued production. If we keep doing the same thing, it will eventually stall the harvest. We don't want to stall the harvest. We have to rotate how we do things. If not, our progress will stall.

> The steps of a good man are ordered by the LORD, and He
> delights in his way.[5]

> A man's heart plans his way, but the LORD directs his steps.[6]

When we begin to walk in the how God has given us, everything that how touches is touched by the supernatural. It begins to
change. It is transformed.

Transformation is part of being in God's purpose.

> But have you not heard? I decided this long ago. Long ago I
> planned it, and now I am making it happen. I planned for you
> to crush fortified cities into heaps of rubble.[7]

⧉ Finding God's "how" comes at a price.

〜〜〜〜〜〜〜〜〜〜〜〜〜〜〜〜〜〜〜〜

🔥 What in my life am I most afraid of losing?

〜〜〜〜〜〜〜〜〜〜〜〜〜〜〜〜〜〜〜〜

PART 7

CRAVEABLE LEADING

*I do not pray for these alone, but also for those who will
believe in Me through their word; that they all may be one, as
You, Father, are in Me, and I in You; that they also may be
one in Us, that the world may believe that You sent Me.[1]*

·

OUR ATTITUDE TOWARD leaders changed somewhere, but
leader worship is nothing new. The Garden of Eden is an
example of how quickly we fall in love with our leaders.
Our choices are often influenced by outside voices of those who
could care less about us.[2] We are people who are too easily impressed.

Now we can "follow" the people we admire every day on Twitter.
Lady Gaga was the most followed person on Twitter in the world as
of this writing, with over eighteen million followers. Justin Bieber
was ranked number two with over sixteen million followers. And
ironically, the only positional leader in the top twenty was Barack
Obama, ranked number eight with over twelve million followers.[3]

You may say, "Yeah, but Lady Gaga and Justin Bieber aren't
leaders." Well, check out how many followers you have on Twitter.
Are you? If you define leadership as influence, then both Gaga and
Bieber are leaders. Maybe they are not the right kind of leaders, but
they lead. They influence what people wear, buy, and even think all
around the world. And their number of followers goes far beyond
how many followers they have on Twitter. It's all just a little bit
scary, don't you think?

Everybody wants to be somebody, and in our minds success (however we define it) makes us somebody. One way we define success is
by how many people listen to us. Whether it is how many people
attend your church or how many "friends" you have on Facebook,

the amount makes you significant, you think. The scorecard for success is measured by the question "How many?"

Jesus was the greatest leader in history. He was concerned (and obsessed) about the "How many?" question. But His vision was incredibly long. He saw far beyond the "How many?" question for next Sunday morning or on the side of a mountain.

If you are making long-term influence criteria for a great leader, He has no rivals as the perfect model. More than two thousand years after Jesus walked on earth, He has over two billion followers, or an estimated one-third of the world's population.[4] Now I admit the word *Christian* is loosely defined by my sources, but I find the long-term popularity of Jesus amazing. The truth is (although this is unlikely), Lady Gaga and Justin Bieber could be an afterthought by the time you read this. You may say, "Who the heck is he talking about?" But when I say "Jesus," you will know whom I am talking about.

Jesus has shaped more lives than anyone in the history of the world. He was and is a craveable leader. Although volumes can be written about why, here are two big reasons. First His influence came from who He was:

> In the beginning was the Word, and the Word was with God, and the Word was God. He was in the beginning with God. All things were made through Him, and without Him nothing was made that was made. In Him was life, and the life was the light of men. And the light shines in the darkness, and the darkness did not comprehend it.[5]

Second, His influence came from how He led. He was a craveable leader who saw beyond Himself to a movement. He knew that the multiplication and empowering of leaders like Him would keep things moving. How did He do it?

28

HE LED OTHERS TO GET IN

*I tell you the truth, anyone who believes in me will
do the same works I have done, and even greater
works, because I am going to be with the Father.*[1]

⦿ Jesus taught others how to
get others in the kingdom.

JESUS ASSURED US that His work and influence would keep going
and get even better! When I look at His life on earth, that truth
is hard for me to wrap my brain around.
Look at all that Jesus did:

- Being craveable to those around Him
- Listening to the Father and understanding His
  mission
- Surrendering His will to God's will
- Finding and training a winning team to replace Him
- Having a team around to help Him
- Loving those no one else would love
- Demonstrating the power of God
- Communicating the purpose of God
- Emulating the person of God
- Recognizing how He needed to get things done

All those great things set the stage for this . . .

GETTING PEOPLE INTO THE KINGDOM OF GOD

Jesus did everything with purpose. He didn't do a bunch of good things for the sake of others thinking He was a good man. His agenda was not to prove He really cared. There's no question people were impressed by the things they saw Jesus do, and they knew He cared about them. But He wasn't about doing and saying things to make a great first impression on people. He had a higher purpose.

Jesus's actions were focused on His mission. His mission was about getting others involved in His mission, not simply making converts. Because of His heart for the harvest, multiplying harvesters was a driving force in His work. His results would be limited if He focused on the number of people He could convert. He had three years to go fast and far. And what about after He died? What then? Furthermore, what about those who didn't accept the message? Below are only a few of those Jesus connected with who rejected Him and His message.

- The rich young ruler—"Disheartened by the saying, he went away sorrowful, for he had great possessions."[2]
- Judas—"He departed, and he went and hanged himself."[3]
- People in Nazareth—"And he did not do many mighty works there, because of their unbelief."[4]
- Pharisees and chief priests—"Search and see that no prophet arises from Galilee."[5]

These are only a few examples of Christ being rejected in the New Testament. And keep in mind that there are thousands more who never made it to the pages of the Bible.

The "followship" of Jesus was terrible at times, particularly around the time of His death. Only a few loyal souls stayed close, including His mother.[6] And let's face it; most of our mothers believe in us even when it's crazy. Does your mother really count? I mean, I know some people who would use their mothers for a job reference if they could get by with it. No disrespect to Mary, but I would have expected her to be around. However, Jesus could not and did not make followers out of everybody.

The point is the message and mission of Jesus was far bigger than Jesus's human existence on earth. Although He was the Son of God, He was still limited by His humanity. And we have the exact same limitations as Jesus did. So His approach to the mission is relevant and precious information to us. We can practice His pattern for helping people find, follow, and be like Him. We have so much to learn from Jesus. His mission was about others:

- Getting in
- Growing up
- Going out

As Jesus went about His mission on a daily basis, He modeled a reproducible plan and pattern for those with Him. His mission would have died with Him if He did everything Himself without leading and training others to do the same things He did. He multiplied Himself through the followers the Father gave Him. He passed His passion on to them for the least, lonely, and lost.

GETTING IN

Jesus was determined to help people get into the kingdom of God. He was willing to die to see it happen. That's really what His entire mission was based around—getting people into relationship with the Father. You see, it wasn't enough that Jesus did part of what God told Him to do. Pouring into twelve disciples or healing sick people was important, but it was all about the mission and getting people into the kingdom of God.

- Impact
- Initiate
- Influence

Jesus was all about people getting in the kingdom. He went from city to city and village to village to find those ready for the kingdom.

In almost every place Jesus was so craveable they would run to get in the kingdom. He took His followers with Him and showed them how to demonstrate why others should believe Him.

When you watch Jesus prepare His followers to carry on His mission, you see an impressive process. Notice the different circumstances they faced with Him (which is limited to a few stories listed in the Bible) during their preparation to impact the world. Sickness, rejection, food shortages, limited funds, demons, death, grief, sex scandals, legal issues, and religious arguments were only a few challenges in the Gospel of John alone. Sounds like either a week in the life of a pastor or a Jerry Springer marathon, don't you think?

Jesus saw long and far. He knew that hundreds and even thousands of converts would never sustain the movement for long. Jesus was preparing His disciples to lead the greatest movement in the history of the world. A vision to multiply believers ("me"), small groups ("we"), and churches ("us") was vital to the future of the movement. And it worked, didn't it? For Artie Davis, Cornerstone Church, and you! Praise God!

So He sent them out to try and do it on their own. He had to demonstrate and train these guys in the whole process. He had ongoing conversations with them about what was happening in their ministry. He would help them discover new ways (hows) to get greater results on His mission. These men with Jesus had to learn fast, because the birth of the church was coming soon and they needed to be well prepared!

---

*Jesus's mission would have failed
had He not multiplied Himself.*

Who can I help to get others in the kingdom?

29

I LEAD OTHERS TO GET IN

For our gospel did not come to you in word only, but also in power, and in the Holy Spirit and in much assurance, as you know what kind of men we were among you for your sake. And you became followers of us and of the Lord...[1]

My good deeds only matter
when done in Jesus's name.

IF HE DOESN'T come through, I am messed up.

Ever feel that way about the people you are doing life with? I hope so. We have to understand we can't help and lead others to be like Jesus without listening and walking in the power of the Spirit.

> I don't want my life to be explainable without the Holy Spirit.
> I want people to look at my life and know that I couldn't be doing this by my own power. I want to live in such a way that I am desperate for Him to come through. That if He doesn't come through, I am screwed.[2]

Saying that what we are doing is "in the name of Jesus" is not the same as actually doing it "in the name of Jesus." I hear people say we are feeding, clothing, educating, healing, and giving water in the name of Jesus, but what does that mean?

Doing good deeds in the name of Jesus doesn't mean we go out and meet needs and say, "We are doing this in the name of Jesus." To do something in the name of Jesus means we are doing it as

Jesus would have done it. Jesus would hear from the Father about where, who, and how. Then He would act or speak for the purpose of bringing someone into the kingdom.

Buying a toy, sponsoring a child, or going to help dig a well is not enough to fulfill God's mission. I know those things are great, and we *must* do them. But all those good deeds must be done with the purpose of moving people to get in, grow up, and go out for the kingdom. Doing good deeds makes us feel better. We think we have made a difference, and we may have for a day or so. But deeds are to be done in the name of Jesus, and that means along with the deed there must be a purpose. What is that purpose? The planting of seed that could bring the fruit of a new person coming to know Jesus.

Think about the time Jesus came to the pool of Siloam. A lame man was there with many others. But only that certain man was healed by Jesus. Many sick people were around, but only one was healed. Why? We can only assume it's because the others were not spoken to Jesus by the Father.

> Do you see that faith was working together with His works, and by works faith was made perfect? And the Scripture was fulfilled which says, "Abraham believed God, and it was accounted to him for righteousness." And he was called the friend of God.[3]

Remember, "Faith comes by hearing, and hearing by the word of God."[4] Abraham heard God, believed that He was going to do the impossible through him, and God established a great nation through him.

Abraham's faith—believing a promise God had given just to him—was not the kind of faith we think about unto salvation. Rather it was faith in God while in relationship with God, and then moving, acting, and speaking in alignment with what God said.

> And whatever you do, in word or deed, do everything in the name of the Lord Jesus, giving thanks to God the Father through him.[5]

Everything we do must be done in the name of Jesus. Listen, that doesn't mean we can just do what we think or feel we should do, and then stamp it with "I did this in the name of Jesus." Doing something "in the name of Jesus" means we do it as His representative because He wants us to. We do or say what He wants. And we do that by hearing from God first and foremost and then doing what He says.

> Therefore, we are Christ's representatives, and through us God is calling you. We beg you on behalf of Christ to become reunited with God.[6]

That means we lead with a Jesus agenda and under a flag of the gospel. We are God's highest-ranking reps on earth. We may bandage a wound or give a bottle of water away, but it is all for Jesus— His fame and His mission. We do it "in Jesus's name."

I think a good example of this is how most believers pray. It doesn't matter what they pray, they add on the end, "We ask these things in the name of Jesus." You are saying more than you think, so be careful. You are saying, "If Jesus was here and He was me in this very place and circumstance, He would have prayed the exact thing!" Can you really say that most times when you pray, Jesus would pray exactly the same way you just prayed?

The "Christian" community has used this phrase as a spiritual metaphor and a standard "close" for all prayers simply out of tradition and habit. Often we have no idea the implications of praying or serving in Jesus's name. God has really been rocking my world with this lately.

Don't say "in the name of Jesus" unless...

- ✦ You know what you are doing is of God.
- ✦ You are responding to a direct command of Scripture.
- ✦ You have heard directly from God and He said to you personally that is what you are to ask for or to say!

Anything else is BLASPHEMOUS!
I know this may be making you uncomfortable, but you really

need to understand this principle. When we say "in the name of Jesus," it means that Jesus has said it, and you are then invoking His authority over what you are speaking. It's like a child who goes to his teacher and says, "My dad said I am supposed to get out of school early." The teacher calls the dad, and the dad is furious because he didn't say that! The father's son was basically calling his dad a liar. He claimed something that was not true.

Read John 14. Jesus says He never said or did anything of His own authority, only what the Father told Him to say or do. So He said, "If you see Me, you have seen the Father!" People are supposed to see Jesus in us the same way! That will only happen as we train ourselves to only do and say what we know God has communicated for us to do—nothing more or less!

So when God says for us to pray for this, that gives us permission to say, "In the name of Jesus." We heard from God. When we say and do what He said, then and only then will we receive the promise: "Ask Me anything in My name, and I will do it."[7] You see that? The only way that works is that Jesus said to do it in the beginning. We are just agreeing with Him.

So if He said He would do it, and we speak and ask in conjunction with Him—*bam!* "In the name of Jesus" means Jesus is "not a man, that He should lie."[8] He will do what He said He would do. "In the name of Jesus" is a powerful phrase. Unfortunately many use it not knowing what they are saying. So if you don't hear it, don't say, "In the name of Jesus."

So when I am with people, I listen and look for the opportunities God wants me to engage in. When I do this in conjunction with listening to God and walking in the Spirit, then great fruit will result.

> Therefore those who were scattered went everywhere preaching the word. Then Philip went down to the city of Samaria and preached Christ to them. And the multitudes with one accord heeded the things spoken by Philip, hearing and seeing the miracles which he did. For unclean spirits, crying with a loud voice, came out of many who were possessed; and many who were paralyzed and lame were healed. And there was great joy in that city.[9]

The first command we have is "go." That is movement. It actually means, "As you go…" Jesus took His followers through a process and modeled the plan for His church to win the world. "For I have given you an example, that you should *do as I have* done to you."[10] What does that really look like?

Impact

What do you have to impact others with? A seed! Yeah, a seed. The kingdom of God comes in seed form. Have you ever tried to make an impact with a seed? Take a corn seed, a single corn kernel. Throw it at the ground and see how much impact it has. None! Unless you are standing in a freshly plowed field and the soil was just turned over and over. If that's the case, take the seed and gently drop it from your side, and voilà! The seed goes deep in the ground, and you can't even see it. Now that's impact!

We need to always be asking God, "Which life around me is being turned over by the Spirit? Whose heart and life are soft enough to be impacted by the seeds of kingdom if I drop them into their lives?"

Initiate

Make the move. Don't wait. Make the call, send the text, and go by that office or house. I always have to make the first move and understand that my efforts for God may not always be received well. But if we walk in the Spirit and listen, no seed will fall on rocky ground. The seed will fall in a place that will produce results.

Invest

This is not a one-time shot. My friend Reggie McNeal calls those attempts to reach people "drive-by shootings." Jesus invested in people, starting with twelve men. This is real-life investment of time, love, energy, and heart in people to whom God sends you. Sometimes those people may disappoint you, but they, like our own children, are worth the investment. The return could be thirty, sixty, or one hundred times what we put in. But the more we invest in those whom God has placed in our lives, the greater the return.

MULTIPLICATION

"Go make" is a verb form meaning the putting together of parts or combining substances. Reproduction happens when the seed of the man combines with the egg of the woman. You "make" a baby! That's multiplication!

The first command to man was to be fruitful and multiply![11] God "seeded" mankind with a male and a female; He provided the two necessary ingredients to carry out their "what must I do" (be fruitful and multiply) and their "what must be done" (fill the earth and subdue it).

No one will "multiply" with you unless you are craveable! I'm sure that's why God created Eve very "craveable" to Adam! I don't mean to sound brash here, but I need to make a point: if you have the seed of the kingdom and want to plant that seed in the life of someone else, don't act like a judgmental jerk. If you do, that seed will bounce off!

There is something about my wife that I crave. When I was dating my wife, I used to ask her this question: "Would it be possible to shrink you up and put you in my pocket? That way, all throughout the day, whenever I wanted to, I could take you out, give you kisses, and then put you back." I know this is a silly little thing, but she was that craveable to me. There is nothing else I'd rather be doing than to spend time with her. Sometimes I just want her to sit by me and not say a word. Her presence is still very craveable to me.

When we got married, it was our desire to reproduce, to multiply ourselves. If we don't multiply, we die! If my wife and I had not been able to multiply, then our family tree would have died with us. This is why the people you impact must also multiply.

> Then the churches throughout all Judea, Galilee, and Samaria had peace and were edified. And walking in the fear of the Lord and in the comfort of the Holy Spirit, they were multiplied.[12]

All living and growing things *must* multiply.

I have to tell you, I love spending time with men and women who are willing to get in, grow up, and go out. I love leaders. I particularly love to lead the leaders at my church. Nothing is more exciting than to see those you are leading follow this pattern. Through the years I've had the privilege of watching many of our leaders grow and then go out.

Over the past three years we've opened two new extension campuses at our church, and we are planning more. This could not have happened if we didn't have men and women who were willing to grow up and go out. Seeing this multiplication is one of the most exciting fruits in ministry.

Lead Like Jesus

> And He spoke a parable to them: "Can the blind lead the blind? Will they not both fall into the ditch? A disciple is not above his teacher, but everyone who is perfectly trained will be like his teacher."[13]

We need to help move people from outside of the kingdom to the inside of the kingdom. "I must help the people who have had a chance to hear the Good News and those who have not."[14]

If we love people—and honestly, most are pretty hard to love—we have to help them find the source of abundant life. There are so many spiritual "options" in the world today.

What exactly separates us from the others? We'll talk more about what this should be later on. It might surprise you.

People Are Searching

> The people saw that Jesus and his followers were not there now. So they got into the boats and went to Capernaum to *find Jesus.*[15]

All of creation is looking to connect with their Creator. It doesn't matter if we deny it; we all know there is "something" greater than ourselves when we look in the mirror. We long to connect with the Creator. So what do I need to do to connect with those who are looking to connect with their Creator? Three actions will influence how effective I will be on God's mission: impact, initiate, and invest.

Jesus had to do this with His own followers. They were with Him for a period of time before they actually "believed" in Him at the wedding at Cana. He asked the Father whom He was supposed to impact, He initiated with them, He asked them to come along, and He invested in them until they believed.

⫸ "In Jesus's name" means when things are done, people move closer to the kingdom.

🔥 How can I more clearly identify my faith in Christ without being a jerk?

30

HE LED OTHERS TO GROW UP

*He serves God by spreading the Good News about Christ. His
mission was to strengthen and encourage you in your faith.*[1]

 Jesus was intentional about others "getting it."

MY COUSIN IRBY was my hero when I was a young boy. He
was ten years older than me and had a muscle car, muscles, and girls. He played in a band, "Al Perry and the
WD Break Downs." He even snuck me in a nightclub once to sit in
the back room with the band!

I remember going into his room one morning before he woke up
and saw that he slept with three pillows, one under his head, hug-
ging the second, and the third between his knees. To this very day I
can't sleep without three pillows!

JESUS HAD TO GROW UP HIMSELF

And Jesus increased in wisdom and stature, and in favor with
God and men.[2]

Jesus experienced firsthand the process of growing up, and so He
understood better how to lead those around Him to grow up.

The impact we can have in the lives of others is incredible.
However, we need to be sure the impact our lives are making on
others has a purpose. We have to see the end of it all. My cousin
Irby's influence on the way I sleep is a great memory, but it will
never change the world. Jesus saw much bigger than just impacting

the way people did things on a daily basis. He was not looking to influence a few for a His lifetime. Jesus saw billions and billions. In fact, He saw us!

Jesus understood His role as a leader very well, and He led with purpose. He was God's master plan, and there was nothing temporary about it. "God saved us and called us to be holy, not because of what we had done, but because of his own plan and kindness. Before the world began, God planned that Christ Jesus would show us God's kindness."[3] Before the world began … Wow! How heavy is that? Jesus was not like us. We roll out of bed one day and decide, "I think I will do this or that for Jesus today—maybe." How did Jesus live out such a big mission and purpose?

Relational Jesus was very relational with those who followed Him. He didn't record His sermon and send it to those who wanted to lead; He spoke with them face-to-face. Now, I'm not downplaying the effectiveness of media or electronic information exchange. It's just that for maximum impact to take place, relationships are best when they are face-to-face.

Intentional

When you are given the task of helping someone move and grow from one place to the next, you can't just throw a penny in the wishing well and hope these new fully grown followers of Jesus just pop out.

Every step of leading His followers to grow up was intentional. He had goals and steps He wanted to see them accomplish.

> And He said to them, "Go and tell that fox, 'Behold, I cast out demons and perform cures today and tomorrow, and the third day I reach My goal.' Nevertheless I must journey on today and tomorrow …"[4]

I heard a great story about a Massi warrior on the Serengeti. Someone asked him how far it was to a certain village. He pointed toward the village and said, "Three looks and two stone throws." He didn't understand a unit distance like miles or kilometers. He measured distance by what he could see with his eyes.

If Jesus was going to be successful in building His kingdom through His church, He had to grow up some guys pretty quickly!

He had the task of taking a circle of simple men and making them into world changers. He couldn't just train these men to do what He was doing; they had to greater things than He did!

This group was the first church. They were going to be given the task of reaching not just Jerusalem, but "all Judea and Samaria, and to the end of the earth."[5] No big deal, right? Yeah, these guys needed to grow up fast!

Have you ever been trained how to do something? Maybe it's how to operate a computer program at a new job or cook a meal from a cooking show you're watching. Anytime we learn something new, it takes repetition and time. We can't perfect or better our teacher without constant contact and training with our teacher.

Growing up takes time. Jesus understood that He couldn't show His disciples how to love or cast out demons one time and expect them to be better than He was at it. Jesus knew they had to "grow up." Just like being trained to do something new, it's a process. Jesus got that.

Just like other leaders trying to help those around Him "get it," He got frustrated with them. Philip asked to see the Father, and Jesus got pretty direct: "You've been with me all this time...and you still don't understand?"[6]

Patience is important when raising leaders, but a hard challenge helps move disciples along! We can't ever give up on those we are trying to help grow up. Jesus never gave up, even on Judas, although there are times He may have thought about it.

Jesus had a clear vision of where His leaders needed to be before He left. That drove Him beyond their stupidity at times. Jesus said, "But the student who has been fully trained will be like the teacher."[7] Can you imagine an army of leaders who were just like Jesus? This worked well in the lives of at least eleven out of the first twelve.

Did it work? Read the Book of Acts and see. The world was turned upside down with all these "little Jesuses" running around. And they reproduced like rabbits at Pentecost and beyond. Dear God, do it again today, just like then!

> Believe me when I say I am in the Father and the Father is in
> me. Or believe because of the miracles I have done. I tell you
> the truth, whoever believes in me will do the same things that

I do. Those who believe will do even greater things than these, because I am going to the Father. And if you ask for anything in my name, I will do it for you so that the Father's glory will be shown through the Son.[8]

These were the actions done how the Father directed them to be done to accomplish the mission.

⧪ He didn't quit until they "got it."

🔥 Whom have I given up on that God
wants me to go back to?

31

I LEAD OTHERS TO GROW UP

We are to grow up in every way into him
who is the head, into Christ.[1]

⬤ I have to help others grow in
obedience to God's plan for them.

I REMEMBER WHEN ONE of my Liberian nephews came to the States for college. He was staying with us for a while and needed to learn to drive. I thought I would be the hero uncle and teach him. I thought, "This guy is twenty years old. Surely he has some understanding of how to drive." Epic fail! He ran over two trees and three bushes just getting out of the driveway!

That first and last driving lesson given by me lasted all of about three minutes. And my final words of instruction were firm and left no room for misinterpretation: "Park it. Now!"

In the kingdom we have a responsibility to help others who are on the journey with us. We don't have the option of telling someone to "park it." Our responsibility is to come along and help lead them on their journey.

My parents tell the story of a time when they were newly married and were "dirt po'." One year the fair came to town, and they so desperately wanted to get in. They didn't have any money at all and couldn't do anything once they got in, but they had to find a way to get in. So they schemed up a plan to go around to the back fence and simply climb over. Their plan worked, and they got into the fair that year.

My parents got in, but that was it. They made it! They checked the box that said, "We went to the fair." Do you think they were able to ride the rides, eat the treats, or play the games? Of course not. All they did was simply get in.

Now I know we can't "jump over the fence" to get in the kingdom the back way. But I think it's important to understand a great truth: it's not just about getting in, but it is also about moving on and leading others to grow up. When I say we need to lead others to grow up, don't let that word *lead* scare you. Leading is just being there. Helping, loving, and giving direction to another is what I am saying. Believe it or not, there are others who can benefit and become better because of you just being you and being there.

Many of us get off to a rocky start on our journey with Jesus. I know I have not only hit but also destroyed many bushes and trees along my path. But I'm glad those around me didn't give up on me. They didn't tell me to "park it," thinking I would never learn how to stay on the path.

You may not see ability in people, but look beyond that right to their hearts (as Jesus did). What God is doing *in* them is as important as what God is doing *through* them in a moment in time. We see more evidence of the disciples' screwups than their wins during Jesus's earthly ministry. But wow, after Jesus's resurrection, things changed.

Permission given to you by another to have impact and influence in their lives is an honoring place. It's a place and privilege that should never be taken for granted. However, many never get to the place where they are genuinely used as the hand of God in a person's life to help mold into the God "me," or the person God planned for them to be.

The reason many don't ever reach that place of influence is because they don't understand what must be done to earn that influence. Influence can't be bought; it must be earned. I would like to add three important elements of influence here that I have noticed in trying to bring about change in anyone, in any situation:

1. Trust

2. Influence

3. Authority

TRUST

The most sought-after, admired, and required attribute of a leader is trust. That should be a no-brainer, but some just don't seem to get it. If someone doesn't trust you, they won't listen or buy into your idea or vision. And quite frankly, trust is one of those things so hard to get but so easy to lose. Have you ever been lost in a town that wasn't your hometown? When you get lost out of town, you want someone who is from the town and knows the town to give you directions. You follow their directions because you trust them. It's the same way when leading anyone. They have to trust us first.

Leading begins with trust. No matter who you are or whom you are with, if you don't have trust, no one will care what you say. Trust is a valuable asset we must guard with great diligence. It is a critical step to being effective in helping others grow through life.

Trust = influence

We must gain the trust of those we are called or intend to help and lead through the process of growing. Trust is the foundation of any healthy relationship we are in.

Trust comes before influence. Leadership is all about influence. Influence gives you the "critical mass" necessary to create movement and momentum with those you lead. Influence comes after and only on the heels of trust.

No trust = no influence

Only after trust is established will you begin to have influence.

INFLUENCE

If you gain someone's trust, they will give weight to your thoughts and ideas. Since they trust you, they will seek out your opinion and input on issues. And with greater trust comes greater influence in larger and deeper matters of the person's life. Go back to being lost. When you find someone you trust and they give you directions, what do you do? Do you argue with them? No! You say, "Thank you," and do exactly what they say. They influence every move you make until you find what you were looking for.

Once a person comes to Jesus, they can't stop there. We have to help them grow in their journey with God. They have to move to the next level of devotion to God in order to become a true follower. That movement comes by our influence.

When we have true influence, other people want to be with us. We need to be craveable to those around us whom we can help follow and grow in Jesus.

We may be tempted to ask the wrong question such as, "How can I get people to listen to me so I can help them?" No. The right question would be, "How can I make myself craveable so they will want to listen to me?" After someone gives us trust and we begin to influence them, we will have the final element—authority.

AUTHORITY

This is what many want! They just want authority handed to them, thinking, "If I'm the boss, they will have to do it." Wrong! When I say trust, influence, and authority, I mean *only* in that order.

I have noticed this most in the leadership arena. If a leader is "put" in a place of authority, it is difficult and takes exponentially more time to gain people's trust and the ability to influence them.

I have noticed in small towns that directions may not come from obvious places. Many times I have gone into convenience stores and asked the person at the cash register for directions. And you know what? Most of the time they don't have a clue! I think, "Man, this is not LA. Do you even live here?" But some little old lady or a man sitting on a bench outside the store will send me exactly where I need to go if I ask.

Authority gives you the ability to make decisions that will affect the outcome of the vision and the team you're leading. Authority should be used as a tool for the movement of the vision. But authority should never be a weapon of reprisal or punishment. If you abuse authority or use it for personal gain, you will soon be without it.

Hmm…What happens if you come into a position where you are given authority and haven't had the opportunity to earn trust and influence? Well, put your big boy pants on. That's a hard assignment and not for the impatient or power hungry. That spot requires humility, love, servant leadership, and patience.

The best scenario is to earn it before you get it. If you get it before you earn it, you will have to pay a higher price. But trust and influence are worth the cost. You will never be effective without them.

Getting in is just the first step. We must move on, grow up, and lead others to grow up.

Brussels Sprout Mind-Set

It's like looking at a brussels sprout (I don't like brussels sprouts) and telling me, "Artie, what's in this brussels sprout is so good for you; you really need it. What can I do to make you like brussels sprouts?" Ha! Absolutely nothing. I don't like them. So if you are convinced I need what is in that sprout, you need to take a different approach to lead me. You need to ask, "What can I give him that has the same benefit as the sprout but is something he really loves?" Now that is the correct question.

Too often we present ourselves as brussels sprouts: "Look at all the great stuff that's in me. Don't you want what I have?" Instead we need to honestly evaluate ourselves and make sure that how we are to others is inviting, loving, and desirable.

I will never be able to help someone follow Jesus if they are unwilling to be with me long enough for me to know them, love them, and understand where they are.

Life is a journey that we invite others to travel with us on. I love the story of Abraham in the Old Testament. I identify even more with him as I get older. God can even use a guy over fifty! Abraham didn't come on the scene until he was in his seventies. God told him, "Leave your country, your people and your father's household and go to the land I will show you."[2]

Abraham listened and obeyed God from place to place. He didn't really know his destination or purpose, yet he just listened to God. Every place he stopped, he would "call on the name of Lord." He didn't know all the answers, he didn't know where he would end up…"so Abram journeyed, going on still…"[3]

Then after a long period of time, Abraham had a frank conversation with God. God told Abraham how He was going to bless and make him great. But Abraham could only think about the fact that he's like a hundred years old now and didn't have a son to carry on his name. Then God called him outside his tent and told him, "Look up at the stars, and count them if you can; so will your descendants be." Then the Bible says, "Abraham believed God."[4]

Abraham believed God was going to do something with him that was literally impossible. And his faith greatly affected those with him who saw his faith and honored him.

What others need to see in us as they journey with us is our pattern of life that follows that of Jesus and Abraham.

1. Listen to God.

2. Follow God.

3. Take others with you.

4. Teach them on the journey.

We probably all know people who come to Jesus, but then it all stops there. Like my parents who climbed over the fence to get in the fair, they are unable to do another thing. But now they feel some type of entitlement as insiders, like, "Hey, I got my pearly gate pass. That's all I need. I'm in, baby!"

Jesus told His disciples, "If anyone would come after me, let him deny himself and take up his cross and follow me."[5] If we "come after," we are in a relationship. Following Jesus is not an option; we must do as He did. People who are with us have to see that we are following Jesus and that we live a lifestyle of passion about the kingdom. We are not moving through life following our own wants and desires. When we live that lifestyle, we fully understand and accept that only in losing our lives will we truly find life.

I can't help others if I don't first gain their trust.

 What attitude, action, or habit in me
might be unattractive to others?

32

HE LED OTHERS TO GO OUT

As You sent Me into the world, I also have sent them into the world.[1]

 Jesus sent out others before they were ready.

I'M NOT THE greatest handyman in the world. My knowledge and skill level when it comes to plumbing, carpentry, and electrical "stuff" are very limited. However, when I was working with my father-in-law, I felt invincible. See, he was the master of all those things. He taught me most of what I know about working with my hands.

I remember walking with him from building to building (he was the head maintenance guy) at their mission station in Liberia. At one place something would need fixing, the next place something would need building, and at the next some gizmo needed replacing. After some time he would tell me to go and "fix this." Well, I had watched him and learned, but doing it on my own was something totally different.

But this one thought kept going through my mind, "If I mess this thing up, Dad can fix it. He can fix anything." So I went about my assignment with confidence not in my ability but in the ability of the one who sent me.

> He who sent Me is with Me. The Father has not left Me alone,
> for I always do those things that please Him.[2]

Jesus instilled that in those who followed Him. He understood, "These guys have to fully embrace the power and call of the gospel.

187

If not, they will stall out when I leave." Jesus had to lead beyond the influence of His physical presence (you might read that again because it is leadership gold). So those following Jesus needed to take ownership and responsibility of the spreading of the gospel.

Vision

Vision is what sustains a movement. As Jesus prepared those with Him to continue the work after Him, He gave them vision. Notice what I didn't say. I did not say He cast vision for them. I said He gave them vision.

That's how Jesus led those with Him to go out and do what He had been doing. "He appointed twelve—designating them apostles—that they might be with him and that he might send them out to preach and to have authority to drive out demons."[3] It would have been pointless to take His followers with Him, teach them, let them watch Him, and not charge them to go do the very thing He was doing.

Demonstration

From the very first day Jesus set His agenda: "Come after Me, and I will make you become fishers of men."[4] You can't catch fish if you don't go out where the fish are. Jesus was talking to fishermen; they knew that all too well. But Jesus said, "I'm going to teach you how to haul in men." They weren't using hooks either. Fisherman at the time could not afford a one-at-a-time mind-set. If they did, they would starve, along with their families. They used nets to haul in large catches! Understanding the vision and purpose is huge, but seeing firsthand how to carry that vision out is better. And owning the vision (enough to be willing to die) causes great movements of God with large nets full of fish for generations to come!

Direction

Then He sent His followers out themselves, two by two, to do the same things they saw Jesus do many times before. They would...

1. Demonstrate whom the people should believe

2. Communicate whom the people needed to know

3. Imitate who the people should be (by doing what they learned from Jesus)

Vision is a God-informed prediction of the future. Did you ever think about that? God tells you what you must do and what must be done. You speak to those around you to help them see the same thing. They speak it to those around them. Then you all go do it together. As the movement gains momentum, those around you find others and reproduce exactly the same thing that God said about the future to you in the beginning.

Vision is not complicated; it is simple. But don't mistake simple as unimportant. Vision is vital to the mission of God. Without vision from God, the vision dies when the leader dies or is no longer present. Vision must be bigger than the leader, or it is not sustainable. Watch what Jesus said: "I must preach the kingdom of God to the other cities also, because for this purpose I have been sent."[5] I have to keep going on and on, reproducing the message and the messengers in other cities. Oh, yeah. I can see it too! Vision gives purpose and direction long term. Jesus said, "Here is My future. God has already told Me, and it is your future too!"

▥▷ Disciples were successful because they owned the vision.

◖ What does God want in the lives of people in my city?

33

I LEAD OTHERS TO GO OUT

"The LORD *your God is giving you rest and is giving you this land."...But you shall pass before your brethren armed, all your mighty men of valor, and help them, until the* LORD *has given your brethren rest, as He gave you.... Then you shall return to the land of your possession and enjoy it.*[1]

⬤ We have to want people to stop
following us and start leading others!

SOME YEARS AGO I really got into rock climbing. The sport presented the greatest physical challenge of anything I've ever attempted. When you climb, you climb what is called a "route." A route is a predetermined course on a rock face and is rated in difficulty from 5.5 to 5.13. When the routes hit the 5.10 level in difficulty, they advance by letter: 5.10b, 5.11c, and so on.

When I first began to climb (mostly on indoor clubs of no more than fifty feet in height), completing a 5.7 was a cause for monumental celebration. I had to train all kinds of muscles, balance, strength, and endurance. However, the most important skill was technique! Knowing how to do the moves was required to get to the next "hold."

I had a coach, Alan, who really helped me a lot. Alan was a young college guy who from the outside looked very unimpressive. I was a lot bigger and a lot stronger (only apparent with a set of dumbbells), or so I thought. Now when Alan took off his coat and walked up to the first route and grabbed the holds, his forearms began to look like a direct helium tube fed those monsters. He suddenly looked like Popeye!

Alan did things that seemed superhuman. He climbed completely upside down and never fell. He did things I struggled with for weeks. One simple little route, just a couple of moves that when hanging on them, I thought, "No man can do this." But Alan did it effortlessly.

He would then harness me up, and I would get to those moves that seemed impossible, and having seen him do it, I would pull it off. My ability was more about his ability. I need to see some things done before I will even try them. But Alan helped impossible things seem possible.

WHAT WOULD JESUS DO?

I never really liked that phrase. That mind-set leaves too much room for interpretation. I have seen so many people in and outside the church harmed so deeply by the "religious" with those judgmental mind-sets! When you can interpret WWJD, it opens the door for us to justify your own righteousness and throw rocks at others.

Ourselves

I think we need to change the way most of us view ourselves and others. The more closely we align our thinking with Jesus's, the better we will be.

We should ask ourselves, WDJD (what did Jesus do)? The question "What would Jesus do?" is way too hypothetical. Jesus demonstrated concrete and measurable actions. Are we doing those things?

+ Loving the least of these
+ Building relationships with those outside the kingdom
+ Building leaders who will change things tomorrow
+ Caring for the sick and orphaned
+ Defending the defenseless

Notice: we should only compare *ourselves* with Jesus, not others with Jesus! And also notice, you can and should constantly access

"Who?" and "How Many?" on these kinds of kingdom behaviors. I just handed you a kingdom scorecard!

Others

When we look at others, we should also ask, WDJS (what did Jesus see)? Do I look at others as Jesus did?

+ Am I crying over their lostness?

+ Do I focus on present failure or future potential?

+ Do I see a miracle in the works?

+ Do I believe the Father can use miracles powerfully?

+ Do I see reality as it exists in the mind of the Father?

Notice: We look at others as Jesus would; we don't look at them to see if they are like Jesus!

How are you doing? How are you looking at yourself? How are you looking at others?

Actually operating the way Jesus did requires a greater level of commitment. This is certainly a lifelong process and not a destination. It's more like a "keep being like Jesus," not a receiving of a diploma "like Jesus."

If you have the heart and passion to really impact leaders, you must have influence with them. You need to know what it takes to earn the right to speak into their lives. I have found that the most powerful and endearing quality a leader needs in order to influence other leaders is...

BELIEF

That may sound simple, but those you influence are desperately seeking someone who really believes in them. It doesn't matter how successful or "green" they are; all leaders need affirmation. They don't want someone who just flatters them or looks to use them in their own vision, but rather someone whom they are drawn to who genuinely cares about their heart and vision.

So if you want to be a leader of leaders, you must believe in others. You must see them as God sees them, through the eyes of what He could do with and through them. You have to speak the truth and life into them. Listen to their story and their heart without thinking how it can fit into your story. Honor their passion by giving them your full attention. Ask questions and listen intently without being distracted by others around you.

I can really speak to this because that was who I was. I would listen to another leader's story and passion, but in the back of my mind I would be thinking, "Hmm, this doesn't fit with what I'm doing. Who else can I talk with?" It took being treated that way by someone else to open my eyes to my own self-centeredness and pride. That wasn't fun!

Another leader wants to see, hear, and feel you genuinely care about them, their heart, and their passion. If they feel you just want to talk about what you are doing and what your vision is without taking the time to really know them or hear their heart, you will have *no* influence with that leader.

This is the challenge: Love other leaders deeply from the heart, guard their vision by honoring them, and believe in them. Genuinely love them. Those who can do that are rare gems! That's why there aren't many leaders of leaders.

Believe in someone the way you want someone to believe in you!

Jesus went out to where the multitudes were. He went into the homes of sinners. Jesus went to find "the least of these" wherever He went. Jesus said, "Go and make followers of all people."[2] It's not enough for someone just to find Jesus and come into a relationship with Him. They must understand that it is a lifetime of helping others get in, grow up, and go out. We can't help someone else go out if we aren't going out.

> And He went up on the mountain and called to Him those He Himself wanted. And they came to Him. Then He appointed twelve, that they might be with Him and that He might send them out to preach, and to have power to heal sicknesses and to cast out demons.[3]

We have to show others what it looks like to follow Jesus. Remember, it's not about your morality! It's not that your morality doesn't matter; it does. But our morality is a response to our love for God, not a welcome mat for others to follow. Jesus had "followers."

Those who followed Him heard Him and learned from Him. We have to display to others what that looks like. And God used His Son to make a movement. Jesus demonstrated what He wanted reproduced. "The Lord's power was with his followers, and a large number of people believed and turned to the Lord."[4]

---

*Part of building God's kingdom
is caring for those who lead.*

How can I bless a kingdom leader this week?

PART 8

CRAVEABLE LEAVING

For God so loved that He gave...[1]

WHEN I DIE, I want to have poured out every ounce of love, passion, and vision in me. Taking it with me will cause it to lose its value. Only what I have given to others will last. Not only are we to live in a craveable way, but we also need to leave this world with a lot of craveable seeds left behind to grow and multiply.

There is no way you can separate the love of God from the generosity of God. Great lovers are great givers, and great givers are great lovers. God the Father gave His Son, and His Son gave His life.

34

HE LEFT A LEGACY

*I am praying not only for these disciples but also for all
who will ever believe in me through their message. I pray
that they will all be one, just as you and I are one—as
you are in me, Father, and I am in you. And may they
be in us so that the world will believe you sent me.*[1]

 Jesus's greatest legacy was His church.

A LEGACY IS "SOMETHING handed down or received from an
ancestor or predecessor."[2] A legacy is generally considered
something given or left behind for you. Something of value
to be cherished as a memory and contribution of your value is a
legacy. People who leave a legacy influence the way the people after
them live.

The greatest legacy Jesus left was His church. His church is His
bride, His most prized possession and the very thing He came to
establish, empower, and enlist to carry out His and the Father's
purposes.

Jesus's church was the only entity Jesus said had the ability to
withstand the onslaught of hell and the power to grow His kingdom.
So the church has the power and blessing of Jesus to be aggressive,
not passive. The church is the proactive, empowered tool of Jesus to
change the world. There is no plan B. The church is the only option
and the best gift of Jesus to over seven billion people on Planet Earth.

The purpose of the church is to build the kingdom of God. In
that purpose there are many callings and plans, but the purpose is

singular: build the kingdom! I'm not telling you what that looks like, neither am I suggesting a particular system or process to get the mission of God accomplished.

What I am telling you is that a church obsessed and passionate about their mission of craveability to a spiritually hungry world will get results. I'm saying the church in all its forms is empowered by the Spirit and has been given the gifts and ability to see the mission fulfilled.

Jesus modeled the plan to win the world through the church.

+ Me — Jesus
+ We — Disciples
+ Us — Followers
+ Out of Bounds

Jesus understood this dynamic and modeled for us the growth and empowerment of the church to reach the world. All great things accomplished come at a great cost. He surrendered His life to the will of the Father. Read below these legacy-building descriptions of how Jesus lived. Ask yourself, "Am I living in a way to leave a legacy as Jesus did?"

"Not my will, but yours be done."[3] That is a hard thing to pray and then even harder to do! Jesus, being perfect, still found it difficult to bend His own will to that of the Father's. Remember, He was "tempted as we are,"[4] so He was tempted to do His own thing!

> Greater love has no one than this, that someone lay down his life for his friends.[5]

> A disciple is not above his teacher, but everyone who is perfectly trained will be like his teacher.[6]

> We should go to other towns around here so I can preach there too. That is the reason I came.[7]

Jesus never stopped moving on His mission. There was always movement. He saw the world turned upside down through the implementation of His plan!

▨▶ Jesus left something that would change the world.

〰〰〰〰〰〰〰〰〰〰〰〰〰〰〰〰〰〰〰〰

🔥 What is my greatest temptation?

〰〰〰〰〰〰〰〰〰〰〰〰〰〰〰〰〰〰〰〰

35

I LEAVE A LEGACY

I have brought you glory on earth by completing the work you gave me to do.[1]

⬤ My greatest legacy will be leaving those behind who are better than me.

I REMEMBER BACK IN college getting my grades, and for one of my courses there was an I next to it. I really didn't know what this was. I went to the professor's office and asked him what the I was for. He said it stood for an "Incomplete." He told me I didn't fail the class, nor did I pass and get credit for it. He said I failed to complete everything required by the deadline. If I completed a paper that he said I had failed to turn in, then my grade would be amended. I did the assignment and later received a B and got credit for the course.

Unfortunately, in life we won't be given the option of completing a task after life is over! We get one shot at this thing called life, one shot at doing all that we have been commanded to do and get done. We won't hear God say, "Sorry you didn't get it done. I'll let you try it again."

BEGINNING

I see in Scripture, and in life itself, a cycle. I see that all things have a beginning. A great beginning starts with vision, passion, and purpose. Then comes building. This is the part that generally lasts the longest, is the most exciting, and is the most difficult. But inevitably there comes a time of breaking. That's when what was begun and built begins to wear out. In some cases it becomes completely broken.

Do you remember the story of the poor widow in the temple giving an almost worthless coin as an offering? Jesus praised her because she gave all she could give. Honestly, I don't think it's about how much we give but rather how much we are holding back. God calls us to hold nothing back. He wants us to go all in.

BUILDING

> "I can guarantee this truth: When you were young, you would get ready to go where you wanted. But when you're old, you will stretch out your hands, and someone else will get you ready to take you where you don't want to go." Jesus said this to show by what kind of death Peter would bring glory to God. After saying this, Jesus told Peter, "Follow me!"[2]

This was Jesus's last personal message to Peter. He was putting the spiritual journey in context. When you are a young and immature Christ-follower, you still have room to do things your way. It's what is expected from a child. When you are young, you can't grasp the concept of denying yourself and living a surrendered life.

Jesus was letting Peter see, "This is what I did. In the flesh, I had no desire to go to the cross and suffer such pain, embarrassment, and shame, but that was the will of the Father, so I allowed Him to take me to a place I didn't want to go. Peter, do you see how I did that? You will have to do the same. *Follow Me.*"

The way I leave a legacy as Jesus did is to allow God to "get me ready" in whatever manner is needed. Then I yield and sacrifice all my fleshly desires and allow the Father to take me by the hand. I follow and trust Him, even to the place I don't want to go.

BREAKING

> I am Jesus, whom you are persecuting. But rise and stand on your feet; for I have appeared to you for this purpose, to make you a minister and a witness both of the things which you have seen and of the things which I will yet reveal to you.[3]

Only in that place of complete surrender will I walk to the place God has for me. There I will make the greatest impact for the kingdom, because only what is done for the kingdom will have lasting impact. All other efforts will not stand. They will be wood, hay, and stubble and will burn over time without eternal pay off.

> Not that we are adequate in ourselves to consider anything as coming from ourselves, but our adequacy is from God, who also made us adequate as servants of a new covenant, not of the letter but of the Spirit; for the letter kills, but the Spirit gives life.[4]

> Then the LORD said to me, "Arise, begin your journey before the people, that they may go in and possess the land which I swore to their fathers to give them."[5]

The Spirit moves others to their next move. It's organic. It's not like a leash but a release.

> So we keep on praying for you, asking our God to enable you to live a life worthy of his call. May he give you the power to accomplish all the good things your faith prompts you to do.[6]

> And we are instructed to turn from godless living and sinful pleasures. We should live in this evil world with wisdom, righteousness, and devotion to God.[7]

AND NEVER STOP MOVING

One famous military phrase from World War II says, "We have to go, but we don't have to come back." It was necessary to keep moving in order to gain ground on the enemy. Like the troops during war, anything that is living and stops moving will atrophy and become weaker and weaker.

In other words, we are never given permission to stop. We must keep moving.

The kingdom is all about movement. As we move together, we will take others with us.

> ...because of the hope laid up for you in heaven. Of this you have heard before in the word of the truth, the gospel, which

has come to you, as indeed in the whole world it is bearing fruit and *increasing*—as it also does among you, since the day you heard it.[8]

He who says he abides in Him ought himself also to walk *just as He* walked.[9]

Whenever God moves, we're supposed to move. I love the story of how God led the Israelites in the wilderness by a pillar of cloud by day and fire by night. Whenever the cloud stopped, everyone would stop. And when the cloud moved, they moved. That's how it should be with us. We should be so close to the cloud of God that we can move with the Spirit with ease.

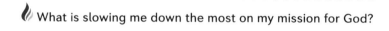

When I demonstrate I'm "all in" with others, they rise up!

What is slowing me down the most on my mission for God?

PART 9

CRAVEABLE US

For the kingdom of God is...righteousness,
peace and joy in the Holy Spirit.[1]

I WOULD RATHER PUT some meat on this issue of being crave-able. We need to be craveable in every context we find ourselves. Another way of saying context would be environment, circumstances, or climate. Many people who follow Christ seem to be the most comfortable and confident at their church on Sunday. They swagger into the church fist-bumping and howling. I like to call that "the home-court advantage." They know the rules, language, and how to score points. And yet think about it a minute. You know whom you are surrounded by on your home court? Yep, that's right, the home team (church people). At least that is the case with most churches in America.

The sad part about the home court of the local church is that it is designed for the home team to be comfortable. So Christians got their swagger on and make their church craveable for home team members while people in the community go to hell.

Even worse, the home team keeps score by the number of people who attend with no concern for who they are. That means the competition is on! We want to have the best church in town, not for the people who are far from God (out of bounds) but so we can kick First Church's butt in an attendance contest. That makes me sick, and I believe it makes God sick too.

There are so many out-of-bounds people in Orangeburg that I am for every church to be full, particularly if they are loving on lost people and preaching the gospel.

You know what I am talking about by now, right? Cornerstone

Church will only be craveable when the people (me included) are living craveable lives. Do you think out-of-bounds people really care how great your preaching and singing is—or even how friendly your church is? I believe strongly in doing all things for God with excellence. But your church can be the "greatest show on earth" and not be craveable. You can miss the reason God sent you to your community. And your "show" can be great to church people (the home team) but boring and irrelevant to those who really need Jesus in your community.

Understanding where God has sent you and how to be craveable in that place is what really matters. My city, my crowd, my church, and my circle all have unique cultures. That makes up your context (place). That is why I can't tell you exactly how to reach people in your area, but the Holy Spirit can and will. We can learn principles from each other, but only God can tell you how you will live out those principles. And in every place you must be craveable to begin to make connection with the people God wants you to touch.

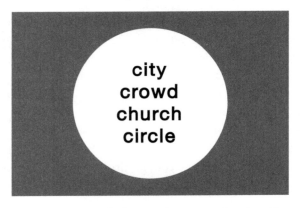

In every context we find ourselves, people should crave the kingdom that we reflect. Remember, perception is king anywhere. What people see, hear, and experience from you forms their opinion about who Jesus really is. I hope you never, ever say you don't care what people think. You should care. Because your life is forming a perception in them, and their perception matters. It matters to the kingdom, and it will make a difference in the lives of many people for eternity. Whom exactly am I supposed to be craveable to? Where am I supposed to be craveable?

36

THE CULTURE MATTERS

*I have become all things to all men, that I might by
all means save some. Now this I do for the gospel's
sake, that I may be partaker of it with you.*[1]

⦿ A church can't be craveable if it is not understood.

ULTURE IS "THE customary beliefs, social forms, and material traits of a racial, religious, or social group; also: the
characteristic features of everyday existence (as diversions
or a way of life) shared by people in a place or time."[2]

Defining culture can be a tricky task, but for the sake of simplicity let's just say culture is the set of "eyeglasses" we see most all
things through. Our culture shapes how we interpret people, actions,
events, emotions, food, entertainment, and more. The eyeglasses of
culture even shape the way we view God, Christians, and church.
That's right. And the views of those things vary dramatically from
Seattle, Washington, to New Orleans, Louisiana, and all the way
to Orangeburg, South Carolina. And in every place, every person's
view of God is affected by us! Does that scare you? It does me. And
it should.

Just understand that when we set out to help people find, follow,
and be like Jesus, how we do that is driven a lot by culture (God certainly knows this). Some people deceptively think that all you need
to do to reach a city is preach the Bible. Are you kidding me? You
do know that some people don't believe in the Bible or even want to
hear what you have to say about it. You can't just go around and say,

"But the Bible says this or that." We are not living in a time where people respect the authority of the Bible.

I am passionate about the Word of God and the authority of Scripture. But the way I present truth at Cornerstone includes an understanding of the world where people live. Culture is not evil, by the way. Culture has evil parts, but it is not evil in itself. The clothes we wear, the things we value, and the way we communicate are all a part of who we are as people. Within culture is where we can discover what God can use to open hearts to the gospel.

Monrovia, Liberia, is a city in Africa that Cornerstone has adopted. We have ties to Liberia. My wife, Georgie, grew up in Liberia, as did her four adopted sisters. Our church is engaged in a humanitarian, faith-based organization called Think Liberia (www .thinkLiberia.com). Needless to say, through the years I have experienced Liberian culture and am passionate about it. I don't speak fluent Liberian English like my wife, but I've been there enough that I can speak in a way that people can understand me.

How I speak and preach when I'm in Liberia is not the same as when I am in Orangeburg, South Carolina. Since I've done ministry in Liberia for over twenty-five years, I understand the nuances and taboos, so I'm able to communicate the Word of God in a way that Liberians can understand.

A craveable church is able to communicate something relevant. What I mean by relevant is something that is useful in everyday life, understandable, and valuable. When you communicate the truth of God, it's simple. Your language must be common and make a direct connection into the world where your hearers live.

The Bible is the most relevant book in history. The original language used to write the New Testament was common, everyday Greek. Common Greek was the language of the everyday people who were the original readers of the Bible. God used ordinary people through the power of His Holy Spirit to write the Bible. He still uses the Bible to speak to ordinary people today. Images and illustrations Jesus used connected with their world beyond the words. Farms, storms, birds, and water were a vital part of life, so Jesus used those images constantly to teach.

The Bible is simple, but that does not mean that it's easy to live by. What is easy is to present the Word of God in a way that it's all mental and intellectual. Providing information is easy, but making application is hard. When I tell you that you need to forgive just as Jesus Christ has forgiven you, that is simple, right? Then when I unpack the truth further to explain if you don't forgive, your Father in heaven will not forgive you, that is simple too. But is it easy to do? No way. But the truth is powerful. When we hear things like "do all things without complaining or arguing"[3]—that's simple, right? But is it easy to do? No.

Desperate people attend our church every single week to give God and church one last chance. They're struggling physically, emotionally, and spiritually. Maybe their marriage is on the rocks, their health is bad, or they are in financial trouble. As they are drowning in life, they are looking up to see if there is a life ring. We must communicate sound, biblical truth in simple, applicable ways. We must place the Word of God on a shelf they can reach. We must consider the culture of our listeners, so they will know we are in touch and have some understanding of where they're coming from. If we are out of touch, they will not listen. Jesus was in touch with the culture of His time; so must we be.

The church needs to be students of the culture they serve so they can communicate. As a pastor, I face a lot of different cultures in Orangeburg. There are not just black and white cultural issues but also numerous subcultures—from the richest to the poorest, from country music to hip-hop art, from country club members to NASCAR enthusiasts.

I am a student of culture. I listen to diverse music styles, read books by many different authors, and go to a variety of movies. I am a student of the Anglo Saxon, white, American culture. I am a student of African American culture and a student of Liberian culture. Culture in America and the world is changing. Culture will always be changing. To reach people in culture, we must understand the times and let God change our "hows" so we can speak to people.

I am a student of culture so that I can more effectively communicate the gospel.

I have to be connected to the same world that my listeners

experience every day. I cannot be a student from the culture one hundred years ago, nor can I communicate in one-hundred-year-old language.

The origin of the phrase "when in Rome do as the Romans do" is not agreed upon by many. Opinions vary, but most agree that it was not evil as some people take it, but the idea is to respect local customs. The idea is captured in the words of the world's greatest missionary—the apostle Paul. Read what Paul said to the Corinthians:

> Even though I am free of the demands and expectations of everyone, I have voluntarily become a servant to any and all in order to reach a wide range of people: religious, nonreligious, meticulous moralists, loose-living immoralists, the defeated, the demoralized—whoever. I didn't take on their way of life. I kept my bearings in Christ—but I entered their world and tried to experience things from their point of view. I've become just about every sort of servant there is in my attempts to lead those I meet into a God-saved life. I did all this because of the Message. I didn't just want to talk about it; I wanted to be in on it![4]

I want to communicate in a way people can understand. If you really care about people, you will put aside your pharisaical attitude and embrace a world needing to understand and to be understood. It is here, with complete humility, that you will find those who are willing to follow Christ. You will be craveable to a starving world, you will make a difference in lives here on earth, and you will bring many into heaven's gate.

When people come into a church environment, they want to hear biblical truths explained and illustrated in a way they can understand. Relevance really does make a church craveable. I'm passionate about helping local churches and Christians become more craveable. You and I need to be craveable because we are the church.

All around us and with us are many circles—circles of strangers. For me to connect in these circles, I need to know who they are and what they love. That is their culture or the world in which they live on a daily basis. I need to know what they eat, who they cheer for, and what they do on the weekends. And it does not need to matter whether I completely agree with some of the things they love for me to love them unconditionally.

How stupid we are for expecting out-of-bounds people to live holy lives and judge them when they do not. I expect out-of-bounds people to be themselves. In fact, I prefer it that way. I want my relationship with out-of-bounds people built on honesty and authenticity. When they are, trust will soon follow. I need to have compassion on the multitudes as Christ did. Christ laid down all pretenses and embraced humanity with humility.

Culture plays a huge part in the effectiveness of how we impact those around us. If we approach someone in an American hip-hop culture and invite them to our "cowboy church," how effective do you think that will be?

WHAT THEY SEE

Context is also vital. Just like culture, the variety of contexts is almost limitless. You have things such as age, education, financial, geographical, sports, gender, and so on.

Look at how Paul helped Timothy prepare to be a missionary in his context. Warning: men, this is going to hurt you. How far would you go to connect with culture in order to be a better witness for Jesus? How about circumcision?

> Then he came to Derbe and Lystra. And behold, a certain disciple was there, named Timothy, the son of a certain Jewish woman who believed, but his father was Greek. He was well spoken of by the brethren who were at Lystra and Iconium. Paul wanted to have him go on with him. And he took him and circumcised him because of the Jews who were in that region, for they all knew that his father was Greek.[5]

Ouch! If Timothy was like most of us, he would have pitched a holy temper tantrum and said, "I don't care what those idiots think! I will just preach the Word whether they accept me or not! I don't care if they are all lost and go to hell."

Did you notice Timothy was already living a craveable life? He was well spoken of by the brethren. Wasn't that good enough? C'mon, Paul! Have a heart, dude. And you know what? Paul did have a heart, and so did Timothy. Their heart was for the people they loved deeply. Jesus died for those people. A little same-day surgery was nothing in comparison. And then people saw their love demonstrated in an extraordinary (and painful) way.

WHAT THEY HEAR

Oftentimes we excuse ourselves from speaking God's words to people. And other times we can be so negative, harsh, and profane that we should not mix blessing and cursing. Some of you I hope never tell the people around you that you follow Christ. All that would do is confuse them because of the way you talk the rest of the time. We can speak the language of culture, but sometimes our words need to be better than culture. Our words come from our hearts. And if our words are ugly, our hearts are ugly. Then we confuse people with our uncraveable lives.

Peter said something to Jesus about the influence of His words. Many disciples were walking away, and Jesus wanted to make sure even His closest followers knew they were always free to go. Wow, that doesn't make business sense, does it? But remember, Jesus wasn't starting a business; He was planting a movement. And for a movement, who is on the ground floor is much more important than how many.

When Jesus told Peter he could leave, Peter said, "Lord, to whom shall we go? You have the words of eternal life."[6] What Peter heard from Jesus changed his life forever. The way Jesus lived gave Him the right to be heard. And Jesus exercised that right!

WHAT THEY EXPERIENCE

People in any culture need to be loved and accepted. Acceptance of a person is not the approval of all the things they love. But the best relationships are placed on a platform of love and respect. When people experience love and respect from me, their view of God is shaped. The same is true when they experience forgiveness and kindness. Everybody in Orangeburg (and your city) needs repeated opportunities to both see and hear the gospel, and that happens through what they experience.

⚡ To be effective, the local church must
be students of local culture.

🔥 What's really important to the people in my community?

37

THE CITY MATTERS

*There is neither Jew nor Greek, slave nor free, male
nor female, for you are all one in Christ Jesus.*[1]

 We need to honor the gatekeepers of the city.

DON'T HATE ON THE HASH!

IN MY HOMETOWN of Orangeburg, in the heart of South Carolina, we have a tradition that started over fifty years ago. There was a man who opened a BBQ house; his last name was Dukes. Now, there are many BBQ spots around most of them carrying the name of Dukes BBQ. Now the most distinctive thing about Dukes BBQ is the hash. Hash is…is…well, it's like a meaty, thick sauce like gravy you pour over rice. Don't ask what's in it; no one really wants to know!

In Orangeburg we take a lot of pride in our homegrown BBQ hash, and if you don't like it, it's best you never say so. Several years ago a pastor was "called in" to pastor a small church near Orangeburg. Those in his newly acquired congregation couldn't wait to take their new preacher and feed him some of Dukes's incredible hash. After going, the new pastor said something along the lines of, "This is nasty. How do you people eat it this stuff?" Well…six months later he was gone! I'm not saying that his disdain of the local cuisine was the sole purpose of his departure, but I'm quite sure it hastened it in some way.

Lesson learned. Know your local culture. If they love hash, you better not hate on it!

WHAT THEY SEE

I wrote an article called "Who Can You Invite to Your Church?" The reason I wrote the article was because I see people come to Cornerstone but not make it their regular church home. Another church is more comfortable for them on a weekly basis. What is funny is that many do come back from time to time. You know why? They come when they have people with them whom their church will not accept. My question for them is, "Why in the world are you going to a church you can't take anybody to?"

A white lady called me once on behalf of her prison ministry to help her with a problem. The problem? Some African American women had gotten saved while in prison, but when they got out, she could not invite them to her own church. She explained that they were not welcome at her church. My question was, "Well, why are you there?"

"They're not welcome there, so can I bring them over to Cornerstone?" she humbly asked.

"You most certainly can! We'll roll out the red carpet, as we do with everyone who walks in our doors." Through the years that's one thing that I absolutely love about our church. Anyone is welcomed there!

I have never met one person in Orangeburg I could not invite to Cornerstone. I know they will be loved and accepted. A lady once said to me, "Pastor, do you know we've got homosexuals in the church?" I threw my hands up and said, "Praise God!" She was shocked!

Not only do I want homosexuals at Cornerstone, but I also want every adulterer, every drug addict, and every alcoholic in our city here. I want every single person who doesn't know Jesus to feel comfortable and accepted coming into this place. Christ didn't come to save those who were well; He came to save those who were sick. If we turn away those who are sick, where will they go to hear about the God who can make them well?

There is a simple reason some people make bad choices: they've never had a group of people show them what it is to be loved and accepted unconditionally. Many people have never had someone speak to them like they were significant.

Perhaps they grew up in a hostile environment, and after leaving home, they never found anyone who made them feel important.

Regardless of the color of your skin, the choices you've made, your socioeconomic status, or your choice of lifestyle, you are important to God and important to us. Can you say that about your church? If not, why are you there? It makes no sense to waste your Christian life going to church with people who are just like you. There is no need for change, no need for compassion, and no room for love

People in churches all over America do not know how to relate to those who make bad choices. The result is that people far from God stay far from God. They believe our opinions are the same as God's. A critical heart shift of understanding the difference between acceptance and approval is essential. Jesus hung out with the prostitutes, tax collectors, and nobodies. He did not approve of their lifestyles, but He loved and accepted them. He genuinely had compassion on them.

A man visiting Cornerstone requested a meeting with me to tell his story. "I'm a homosexual, and I have a live-in partner," he said. He told me he had been kicked out of his last church. Then he asked, "If I came here, would I be welcomed?"

I said, "Not only will you be welcomed, but also you will be loved." I explained to him that he could not join the church or hold a position of leadership, but we would be thrilled for him to get involved in other ways. I assured him I wanted him to come, get involved in a small group, and serve.

WHAT THEY HEAR

> Therefore those who were scattered went everywhere preaching the word. Then Philip went down to the city of Samaria and preached Christ to them. And the multitudes with one accord heeded the things spoken by Philip, hearing and seeing the miracles which he did. For unclean spirits, crying with a loud voice, came out of many who were possessed; and many who

were paralyzed and lame were healed. And there was great joy in that city.[2]

A couple of the leaders at Cornerstone took this man under their wing. They showed him love and acceptance God's way. Guess what? God changed his life. When God changed his life, God changed his lifestyle. That is the way it always works. He came to me eight months after he started attending our church to tell me what happened in his life. He said, "Pastor, I want you to know I've asked my live-in partner to move out, and I understand that is not the best lifestyle for me. I've turned things around, and I want to thank you for having a church that loved me the way that I was."

Notice he said *was*. His story reminds me of what Paul told the church in Corinth. Corinth was an incredibly corrupt but important city. Corinth was also God's city. God's church was making an incredible difference in the lives of people there. How do I know that? Look at who was in the church. Apparently a large group of the members of First Church Corinth had pretty dark pasts. Many were in recovery from something (sounds like Cornerstone), yet there was plenty of space for grace.

Paul told great stories of God changing people:

> Do you not know that the wicked will not inherit the kingdom of God? Do not be deceived: Neither the sexually immoral nor idolaters nor adulterers nor male prostitutes nor homosexual offenders nor thieves nor the greedy nor drunkards nor slanderers nor swindlers will inherit the kingdom of God. And that is what some of you were. But you were washed, you were sanctified, you were justified in the name of the Lord Jesus Christ and by the Spirit of our God.[3]

People in your city need to hear and see stories of the power of God changing lives. The power of a changed life is the greatest evidence that God is real. But changed lives also make the gospel and gospel people craveable.

WHAT THEY EXPERIENCE

What powerful words: "And that is what some of you were." God has called us to accept but not approve. You can accept someone and not approve of their decisions. You can accept and love someone unconditionally because Jesus did that for you. Scripture says that while you were yet an enemy of God, He gave His life for you.[4] Do you think He approved of you being an enemy of His? No! But He gave His life, and He died for you. He died for you with no assurance you would ever embrace Him or His forgiveness. That was an incredible risk! Did you ever think of it that way? Those at Cornerstone who invested in the homosexual had no guarantees that he would ever embrace Christ. They did not use manipulation but loved him long enough to give him a chance to find and follow Jesus.

You need to practice unconditional acceptance and love. People in your city need to experience it from you. And Jesus Christ, the Son of the living God, proved His acceptance and love though His voluntary death.

> Very rarely will anyone die for a righteous man, though for a good man someone might possibly dare to die. But God demonstrates his own love for us in this: While we were still sinners, Christ died for us.[5]

⚡ We are called to reach the *whole* city, not just parts.

🔥 What group of hurting people in my city needs more of my attention?

38

THE CROWD MATTERS

*Keep open house; be generous with your lives. By
opening up to others, you'll prompt people to open
up with God, this generous Father in heaven.[1]*

⊙ The crowd my life touches contains
the ones I'm supposed to reach.

MY LIFE TOUCHES their lives every day even though I
may not know it. They may be one of my hundreds of
Facebook friends, but I know little about them. To be
honest, what they ate for lunch or the funny thing their preschooler
did is hard for me to care about. And I know it is impossible to care
like they deserve to be cared about.

I am talking about my crowd—the crowd I live, work, and play
with. Jobs, grocery stores, PTA meetings, and neighborhoods make
up the masses of people in my crowd. In those masses are specific
people God has planned for me to reach with the gospel. So how do
I (forgive me here) "sort out the bodies."

God puts me in crowds constantly. Most of them are drowning
spiritually and are in desperate need of rescue now. How do I choose
from a crowd that is too big to save? We get close enough to them to
possibly impact or influence, but here it comes again. Craveability is
the key. What makes me any different from the crowd they live with
every day. What distinguishes me from the people they live, work,
and play with? Jesus Christ living in me is the right answer. The craveable me being like He!

We are to live like Jesus. What did Jesus do? He sorted through the crowds, and He looked for crowds to sort through. Buried in those crowds was precious treasure, people for Jesus to "seek and save." What is your "what" or mission? It is the same as Jesus's what: to seek and to save. "Oh, no," you say, "only Jesus can seek and save." Yep. And where is Jesus? Jesus is in you wanting to do what Jesus does. So if your "what" is not the same as Jesus's "what," you are in open rebellion against Him.

I dare you to walk through your neighborhood this week and declare, "I have come to seek and to save you people." I know they will think you are crazy, and I am joking to make a powerful point. I do not want you thrown in jail or a mental hospital on account of me. Your "what" is identical to Jesus's what. Don't resist it; fully embrace it!

So how do you work through helping people in your crowd?

IMPACT

First comes impact. We can have impact without knowing it. People whom we don't even know are watching us and taking notes. That is exciting and scary at the same time. Impact is what one car does to another at a traffic light if they do not stop. That is not the idea we are looking for, but Jesus often stopped crowds in their tracks with the way He lived and spoke.

Everything I do every day impacts someone in my crowd. That statement belongs on your bathroom mirror (and mine). When I impact, I am planting kingdom. I may not even know the people yet whom God has planned for me to reach, but I am impacting them. Zacchaeus watched Jesus in His crowd from a tree when Jesus did not know it.[2] The woman with an issue (of blood) fought through His crowd long before Jesus knew.[3] Jesus impacted them before He knew them.

> Impact—Sowing seeds of the kingdom on the "good ground"
> in the life of another, over a period of time, that produces
> good fruit

INFLUENCE

Influence happens as God gets your attention through specific people in your crowd. At first it may seem like no big deal. A new person moves into your neighborhood with kids the same age as yours. Someone gets promoted to your team on the job. You connect with a foursome of people you have never met before on the golf course. And small conversations and relationships begin.

If you are listening to God, He will begin to show you the people in your crowd He has planned for you to reach. Let God figure it all out, but be sure you "get it" enough (like Jesus) to be seeking and saving. Influence happens over time with repeated connections in the normal traffic patterns of your life. At first these meetings may seem like mere coincidence. But you know better. This is exactly the way the Father works.

> Influence—Watching for God to move certain people to the front of your crowd for you to help find Jesus over time

INVEST

How exciting is it to be used by God to impact and influence people? You would think that is enough and more than most ever do for Him, but He has bigger plans. The impact and influence level is where we help people find Jesus. But remember, God wants us to help people on a deeper level to follow and be like Jesus.

To help people follow and be like Jesus takes you to invest. The word *invest* gives you a word picture that we normally fly over. "To invest" is from Latin origins and describes a garment you know as a "vest." What does a vest do? It wraps around your body, of course, quite closely, in fact. God has a group of people for you to literally wrap around and get very close to. In that process they become your circle and you do life with them.

Jesus had incredible impact on Zacchaeus and the woman with the issue of blood, but to our knowledge He never did life with them on an ongoing basis. He did not even want that because He knew their greatest place of influence was to stay right where they were. He wanted them to establish their own crowds and circles. They needed to help people find, follow, and be like Him.

Invest—People God brings into your life whom you wrap around with time and energy to help them follow Jesus

INVITE

So God gives us people He has planned for us to reach. Some we will impact whom we may never know or barely remember. Others we will influence. For a season we will work with them, live in their neighborhood, or play golf with them. Even others we will invest in may be in a small group.

The final level is those we help be like Jesus. Jesus had Peter, James, and John as His inner circle. Your "invite" group is small. Included are the people who live under your roof. The messiest of all relationships can be where you make the biggest impact on the world. They see you as you really are—warts, scars, and all. The biggest mistakes and failures of your life are in their clear view. And how you process your life with Jesus in light of all these things is what either makes Him craveable to them—or not. They are your spouses, sons, daughters, and more.

There is a circle outside our families that God has planned for you to reach. Oftentimes they follow through the first three levels with you: impact, influence, and invest. But God has bigger plans for your relationship with them. These people will be part of your spiritual legacy. From this group come people who will eventually do things better than you but all for Jesus.

Invite—The smallest group of people who see you up close, over a period of years, and who God has planned for you to help follow and be like Jesus.

On every level it all comes down to what people see, hear, and experience through us.

Live wisely among those who are not believers, and make the most of every opportunity.[4]

...that the sharing of your faith may become effective by the acknowledgment of every good thing which is in you in Christ Jesus.[5]

…or steal, but must show themselves to be entirely trustworthy and good. Then they will make the teaching about God our Savior attractive in every way.[6]

+ We help people find Jesus.

+ We help people follow Jesus.

+ We help people be like Jesus.

I constantly look for opportunities to engage and impact people.

How can I become more aware of people in my world who need Jesus?

39

THE CHURCH MATTERS

*...having favor with all the people. And the Lord added
to the church daily those who were being saved.*[1]

🔘 My church needs to help people
find, follow, and be like Jesus.

WE NEED TO look at the Mission Matrix again in the context of church. Can you see how this works? You can use the matrix as a tool to measure how people are moving forward in your church environment. You can ask yourself key coaching questions as you lead in whatever area.

How's business? God has you in the business of church to get results, not just to sponsor programs. How many people are you helping? What steps can you take to keep people moving?

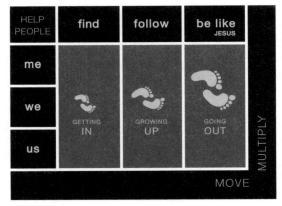

If you had to describe your church to someone, what would you say? Would you try to use language they could understand? I think it's important to use terms others use or hear on a regular basis.

I ran across a church that described themselves as "an urban, multigenerational, and multiethnic church striving to be an incarnational presence in a postmodern and post-church culture."

What? I'm a Christian leader, and I don't think I fully understand all that. Come on! If I were an unbeliever, new believer, or old believer with less than two PhDs, I wouldn't know what kind of church this is.

We try to impress our peers way too much. Our passion should be focused on becoming more craveable for people who are out of bounds. Who cares if some preacher a thousand miles away from Orangeburg is impressed with all my code words. The kingdom gets no benefit by that.

I know the pastor from the church I described. It's a good church, but don't try to fit every "hot" term in your description. We confuse people enough with other things. Let's not start to splinter the church so much that no one can tell you are even a "real" church.

We can understand, operate, lead, and live missionally. We can teach and model a life that is incarnational. We can and should be multiethnic in our church composition. But I think it's better to use simple language and simple illustrations to define our vision and goals.

Getting too fancy on the verbiage just brings confusion. So I would challenge you, when speaking about your church, to use simple language and terms. It brings more unity and understanding to those around you.

Many churches waste their time arguing over all the wrong questions. If what you really care about is the people in your community, you will wrestle, pray, and cry constantly about two questions:

1. What are we doing?

2. How are we doing it?

I think the illustration below might help you talk, think, and pray through what really needs to happen for God to use you. Remember:

+ *Me = you*
+ *We = your small group*
+ *Us = your church*

God communicates to lost people through all three platforms. People see, hear, and experience God. They hear and see the gospel of Jesus Christ. When God is really working in your life and the lives of people around you, the gospel becomes craveable.

Outside	See	Hear	Experience
Me	The power of God: life with them	The purpose of God: my God stories	The person of God: the gospel of Jesus Christ
We	The power of God: life with others	The purpose of God: our God stories	The person of God: the gospel of Jesus Christ
Us	The power of God: life in larger groups	The purpose of God: larger group God stories	The person of God: the gospel of Jesus Christ

ME GOING OUTSIDE

As we flesh out the idea of the church of "me" and put this all together, it should look something like this:

They see me demonstrate the power of God.

What does it look like to demonstrate the craveable power of God? Here are eight things they will see (there are more):

1. They see me being with them.

2. They see me loving and caring for them.

3. They hear me speak of their potential.

4. They hear about the person of God.

5. They hear God's plan for them.

6. They experience unconditional acceptance.

7. They experience real friendship.

8. They experience Jesus through me.

WE GOING OUTSIDE

The beauty of being a Christ-follower to those outside is the way we "do life" together in smaller groups. But smaller groups have the wrong picture of doing life. That stinks—literally. They become so focused on each other they ignore their real purpose: to help people find, follow, and be like Jesus.

Other groups attempt to make "doing life" mean more than talking about deep God stuff and looking at each other once a week in someone's living room. They decide to do a "make us feel good about ourselves" mission project. They make a meal for homeless people or fix a little widow lady's shutters on her house. Then they go to the local Burger King afterward, eat a Whopper with extra cheese, and admire the heck out of each other. Yuck!

If God has given "me" a mission, then God has given "we" a mission.

A smaller circle must have "mission with intention." The idea and spirit of the random mission project is sick unless your "we" has an intentional mission. A group of individuals who come together with the intention of helping people to find, follow, and be like Jesus is what the "we" is all about. The purpose of the "we" is not merely to do life together or to do mission projects together. We do mission together in order to help connect those outside with Jesus.

Should the "we" love and serve each other? Absolutely! That is biblical! But to stop loving and serving each other is unbiblical. We love and serve other people outside the same way we do each other so they can see, hear, and experience the craveable Jesus in "we."

US GOING OUTSIDE

The mission and shape of the church was established when Jesus ascended to the right hand of the Father. Jesus demonstrated, modeled, and taught His followers how the church should function. He taught them what they had to do and what had to get done. Then He taught them how to find "the how."

Churches today are always looking for the greatest and newest "how" to grow numerically, "how" to make the greatest impact, "how" to find leaders, and more.

> "Look!" he said. "The people are united, and they all speak the same language. After this, nothing they set out to do will be impossible for them!"[2]

God was disappointed with their motivation to make a name for themselves. But He openly applauded their system for accomplishing their task. Their system was so good that God said if they continued to work that way, they would have accomplished the impossible. Wow! I like a system like that! It's quite simple, though:

1. Find the right place

2. Find the right people

3. Have a solid vision

4. Be united behind the vision

5. Speak the same language (terms, clarifying wins and understanding the next steps)

I love discovering proven systems to address the challenges of reaching people through the "us." The people at Babel impressed God with the possibilities of what they could accomplish when working together. How much more could His church do to reach every man, woman, and child with the gospel? We have His Holy Spirit. The people of Babel had the potential to do the impossible without Him! I want results for God (and so does He, by the way). His plan for us is to get them.

Look again at the five characteristics of a system that works. Compare the list to what you are doing now. How do you measure up? How many steps in process do you have in place? How many are you lacking? Which one is the most challenging?

The church—me, we, and us—have to first understand "the what." What the church—me, we, and us—must do is simple: help people find, follow, and be like Jesus.

What must be done is simple: make followers who make followers who make followers (multiplication).

> Then the churches throughout all Judea, Galilee, and Samaria had peace and were edified. And walking in the fear of the Lord and in the comfort of the Holy Spirit, they were multiplied.[3]

> "...by stretching out Your hand to heal, and that signs and wonders may be done through the name of Your holy Servant Jesus." And when they had prayed, the place where they were assembled together was shaken; and they were all filled with the Holy Spirit, and they spoke the word of God with boldness.[4]

> But there was a certain man called Simon, who previously practiced sorcery in the city and astonished the people of Samaria, claiming that he was someone great....Then Simon himself also believed; and when he was baptized he continued with Philip, and was amazed, seeing the miracles and signs which were done.[5]

A local church must be craveable! And what made them craveable ten years ago may be making them detestable now. They have become a "smokehouse" for out-of-bounds people.

WHAT THEY SEE

An African American church planter recently posted this on his Twitter feed about his church: "Man, [our] church is just dope! Amazing worship, cake for meet and greet, souls saved and peeps joining the church! Love this church!" Have you ever referred to your church as "dope" and "cake"? I seriously doubt it. But to those in his church and culture that speaks volumes.

In the old days people used a smokehouse to preserve meat. After the people killed an animal and dressed its meat, they stored it for the smoking process that would preserve it. Meat that was properly dried out with smoke and salt could last for years. Remember, there was no refrigeration back then. When the meat dried out, you would have something like jerky. Now don't get me wrong; I like jerky, but it's hard and tough to chew. I don't think we need to be serving up jerky in the church.

Those just hanging in the church are like dried-up jerky. Like meat, they have hung in the church for years. There's nothing craveable about dried-up "jerky Christians." That is what most of our churches are serving these days, just plain old dried-up jerky Christians, no sauce with that, no butter, no spice, just plain old dry!

Now there is a difference between fire and smoke. Firing a piece of meat is like grilling. After meat is grilled (if you are as good at it as I am), it becomes juicy, and wonderful, delicious flavors come out that you won't taste with jerky.

In order for our churches to be craveable, we need to put some fire in them. Do you remember how the movement started? Here is a hint: it did not start with smoke but with fire:

> Suddenly a noise like a strong, blowing wind came from heaven and filled the whole house where they were sitting. They saw something like flames of fire that were separated and stood over each person there. They were all filled with the Holy Spirit, and they began to speak different languages by the power the Holy Spirit was giving them.[6]

Remember, these are the people who found favor with people. They were craveable because the fire made them that way. Like a big, fat, juicy steak off the Artie Davis grill! Come on over. I will fire that baby up right now!

WHAT THEY HEAR—US HELPING PEOPLE FIND JESUS

You hear so many saying, "We are an Acts church." No! That was *their* "how," not ours and not yours. Ever hear a church leader say, "This is just how we do it"? Those words mean certain death! It means they have dropped anchor in deep mud. It's easy for a church to fall in love with "the how." They get in a rut with style, location, systems, presentation, and expectations.

God gave me some fresh bread about the issue of the "how." King Solomon had already proven that he was the right man for the job.

Although not perfect, "Solomon loved the Lord, walking in the statues of David his father."[7] King Solomon had not only succeeded but also showed great promise to do even greater things.

God asked Solomon a question all of us would love to hear: "Ask what I shall give you." What? Did I read that right? Did God just give Solomon a blank check? Wow, my list would have been long. I am afraid it might be the adult version of what I used to send Santa Claus. But the great King Solomon turned it back to God and went into detail about how God had blessed him so much already. He explained how he appreciated how God had loved and cared for him and his father, David. Great leaders have great humility before God, and you can see it all over this story.

Then a dramatic shift came in the conversation. This is when I jumped out of my chair so high I think I hit my head on the ceiling! Solomon said, in essence, "Lord, You have put me in a great position to lead these people, and I appreciate it, but I am young and with no experience...I do not know how to go out or come in."[8]

Did you see what I saw? Solomon told God, "I know the 'what,' which is to lead the people in into your purposes. But I am young, and I don't have a clue for the 'how.'" So we pick up where Solomon asked God to give him the how:

> Give your servant therefore an understanding mind to govern your people, that I may discern between good and evil, for who is able to govern this your great people?[9]

God was so pleased that Solomon asked for the "how" that God gave him everything else too. Do you want your "us" to be used and blessed by God incredibly? Make sure you and all the people in the "us" clearly understand and accept God's mission, or "the what," for your community. "The what" is to help people find, follow, and be like Jesus. Then humbly ask God for "the how." You are not smart enough to know without Him. When you figure that out, you will have the breakthrough for God you long for. You will please Him when you do and be blessed beyond your dreams.

When a pastor, father, leader, or friend asks God for "the how," it changes everything!

WHAT THEY EXPERIENCE

All the time the culture and context of all the people around our "us" changes. In fact, change is the only thing you can really count on! So if people change but the church refuses to change, then the church loves their "how" more than people. And sadly, too many America churches fall into that category. What do they need to experience through our "us"? People who are ready to come to meet out-of-bounds people in their world instead of always insisting that they enter into our Christian Disney Worlds.

> A new commandment I give to you, that you love one another;
> as I have loved you, that you also love one another. By this all
> will know that you are My disciples, if you have love for one
> another.[10]

**⫸ My "we" and I need to move people
to the local church (my "us").**

⫷ How am I helping connect people to my "us"?

40

THE CIRCLE MATTERS

As iron sharpens iron, so a man sharpens
the countenance of his friend.[1]

⊙ If I start with the wrong people, I
will end up in the wrong place.

PEOPLE NEAR YOU are like magnets; they all push you or pull against you. After first coming into a relationship with Jesus, I had great passion and joy. But after a while I became "the backslider." Have you ever been in that place? Most of us have. I really didn't like that place, but I felt trapped at the time. Most of my friends had moved on to college or out of town. Lonely and out of place, I searched for a new circle of people who would make me feel loved and accepted. And sure enough, there is always a circle that will welcome you if you look hard enough. But as happens most of the time, I found the wrong circle!

GOD'S PLAN

God has a plan for the expansion and health of His kingdom. When we become part of that kingdom, we are commanded by God to take an active role in that plan. Our assignments are the same but yet different. We all are called to be like Jesus and help others to do the same. However, each of us is in a different context, with unique gifting and abilities. So God has a plan for us individually.

GOD'S PEOPLE

The first step God uses to get us ready to do what He wants is to put people in our lives. As strange as it sounds, the right people come before anything else. Right people walk with us to do what God has called us to do.

Even though God puts people in our lives, so does Satan! Yes, God puts people around us to push us, stand with us, and help us. But Satan also puts people in our lives to pull us back, pull us away, and try to thwart the plan of God for us. Satan sees great damage to his kingdom and mission at the hand of an empowered, surrendered warrior of God. He wants to keep people far from God, so he doesn't stand idle and let you get stronger. He engages others around you to stop or slow your mission.

This is the kicker: God and Satan put people around us, but we choose who will be with us. *Those we choose to be with us become the circle.*

We have to make the choice about who comes close enough to be in our circle. Our circle is made up of those who are close enough to push us or pull us. They can speak into our hearts. They carry heavy influence with our direction and emotions. We will turn to the left or to the right based on who is in our circle.

Professor Robin Dunbar from Oxford University has researched the issue of influence. He delves deeply into the number of trusted relationships humans can maintain throughout life. We tend to have five best friends, fifteen good friends, fifty close friends and family, and one hundred fifty total friends.[2]

Our circle, our closest teammates, will make or break our mission (the five or the fifteen). We must choose in the Spirit and with great wisdom.

GOD'S PLACE

I believe we won't make it to the place God wants us without first having the right people with us. Think that through: people come first. When we get to the place God wants us to be, we will immediately need those who are with us. Very early in Jesus's ministry He picked His team. He refused to do life or ministry alone. Check it out in the Gospels. Only Luke has Him doing any significant public ministry before He started team building. And although He may not have picked the brightest or the most obvious, He did pick the best to be with Him.

Picking a circle makes so much sense. You need the accountability and support, but also because life is bigger than you are, you need to reproduce yourself. The mission of God is at stake. Your circle helps you not only live well but also serve Jesus well. You need a group of people to watch your back. And you need a team because they need somebody to watch—a model and an example of how a Christ-follower is supposed to live. That's you!

GOD'S PURPOSE

Once we have the right people and we're in the right place, we begin to accomplish God's purpose. We will see and hear God move in ways we never thought possible. I think a good illustration of this is Joshua and Caleb when taking the Promised Land.

God had a plan to deliver His chosen people, the children of Israel, from bondage, but they didn't have the right people to lead. So God let them grow and multiply in Egypt. And when they were finally freed from their bondage and stood at the edge of the land God wanted to give them, those who were leaders among the people failed! They gave fearful and dreadful reports among the people.

Two leaders—Joshua and Caleb—who were on the forty-day trip to spy out the land saw something different than what the others saw. You need these kind of leaders in your circle. Moses and Aaron had raised them up. Joshua and Caleb said to the people:

> Only do not rebel against the Lord. And do not fear the people of the land, for they are bread for us. Their protection is removed from them, and the Lord is with us; do not fear them.[3]

I want men of vision and courage like Joshua and Caleb in my circle!

But the bad leadership outnumbered the good, and the people rebelled. Therefore those leaders were not the right people. Moses made some bad choices. The tragic result of poor leadership was that God's people wandered in the desert for forty years until the wrong people died. Even Moses did not make it in, but guess who did? You're right; my boys Joshua and Caleb. Keep those "bad report" people out of your circle. The story is full of great leadership lessons and warnings. See the entire episode in Numbers 13–14. Your circle would benefit from a close study of what real leadership looks like.

Only in God's plan, with God's people, and in God's place did the people see the power of God move for them to take what God had promised—their own land!

GOD'S POWER

When the nation of Israel crossed the river into their own land, God said, "I will go before you. I will drive out all your enemies, and every place you set your foot will be yours."[4] Now that's a conquering God!

We need others with us who are actually better than us. I still can't wrap my brain around the fact that Jesus told His circle (and us), "You will do better than Me at this," when He predicted "greater things."[5] If you heard Him say that, how would you have responded? In all due respect to Jesus, I would have laughed out loud. The Bible doesn't tell us how His circle responded, but if anyone laughed out loud, it was Peter, no doubt. "You got to be kiddin' me, Lord; really? That's just wrong, Lord." But we can't be intimidated by that thought; we must intentionally lead believing what Jesus said. We will be better than Him at this!

JESUS'S CIRCLE DID BETTER

When you are with people who aren't good at something, it makes you feel as if you are good at it! I was reminded of this recently when trying to learn to swim laps in the pool. Everyone there was better than me! I hated that! I felt like a doofus. There's nothing like experiencing humiliation and drowning at the same time.

I thought, "Where are the people who are bad at this like I am?" I want to think I'm getting better, and I'm not "feeling" that while next to the "experts." Well, feelings are deceiving. The truth is, those around me were kind enough to recognize my struggle. They provided very helpful instruction and encouragement. In this humiliating stage of failure and constant challenge, a strong leadership principle comes to light: *if I'm not with those who are better than me, I will never get better.*

Jesus's circle grew to do even greater things than He did because they were with Him for three years. They watched Him do well at the things that they were terrible at. And Peter was bad in ways as I was bad in the pool, like that day when he tried to walk on the water just as Jesus did.[6] At least I didn't sink. But Jesus was the expert who picked Peter up. Peter had the right circle for sure!

Who are you learning from? Who is speaking life, hope, and challenge into your life? Are you really seeking to be better from those who are better?

> Jesus (the one we call Justus) also sends his greetings. These are the only Jewish believers among my co-workers; they are working with me here for the Kingdom of God. And what a comfort they have been![7]

You have to be with someone for a while and see them in action in different situations to really know what they are like. So if you want to know who I'm like, it takes time. You need to know me pretty well.

Have you ever had one of your friends or relatives say, "You act just like your daddy"? That may or may not be a compliment, but apparently they know you and your father well enough to draw the comparison. And when we are like our Father God, we will become over-the-top craveable.

⟋⟍ Only the right people will help me
accomplish all God has for me to do.

❦ What people in my world are hurting
my ability to do God's will?

NOTES

Introduction: Understanding Craveable

1. Maureen Mackey, "Apple: The Power and Profit Behind 'Simple,'" TheFiscalTimes.com, May 1, 2012, http://www.thefiscaltimes.com/Articles /2012/05/01/Apple-The-Power-and-the-Profit-Behind-Simple.aspx#page1 (accessed September 21, 2012).

2. 2 Corinthians 2:15–16, The Message.

3. See John 14:6.

4. Luke 10:3.

5. John 12:32.

6. John 14:9, cev.

7. Luke 17:9, nlt.

8. ThinkExist.com, "Dr. Seuss Quotes," http://thinkexist.com/quotation/ today-you-are-you-that-is-truer-than-true-there/411469.html (accessed September 21, 2012).

9. Colossians 4:5, ncv.

10. Acts 2:46–47.

Part 1: Craveable Perception

1. 1 Peter 2:21.

Chapter 1: Perception Rules

1. Matthew 13:14, nas.

2. Dictionary.com, s.v. "perception," http://dictionary.reference.com/browse/ perception?s=t (accessed September 24, 2012).

Chapter 2: What You Believe

1. Isaiah 43:10–11.

2. Proverbs 23:7.

3. 2 Chronicles 16:9, ncv.

Chapter 3: We Do What We Believe

1. Dave Gibbons, *Xealots* (Grand Rapids, MI: Zondervan, 2011), 32.

2. Rick Warren, *The Purpose-Driven Life* (Grand Rapids, MI: Zondervan, 2002), 237.

Chapter 4: We Say What We Feel

1. Proverbs 29:11.

2. Luke 6:45, nlt.

3. Proverbs 4:23, nlt.

Chapter 5: We Display What We Want

1. Proverbs 20:11.

2. 2 Corinthians 9:7.

3. Guy Kawasaki, *Enchanted* (New York: Portfolio/Penguin, 2011).

CHAPTER 6: BEING WITH US IS AN EXPERIENCE!

1. 1 Timothy 4:16, THE MESSAGE.

PART 2: CRAVEABLE LISTENING

1. Luke 6:40, NIV.

CHAPTER 7: HE HEARD THE VOICE OF THE FATHER

1. 2 Peter 1:17–18, NCV.

2. See John 8:28.

3. See Acts 16:6–7.

4. See Mark 1:35; Luke 4:42.

5. John 5:30, NIV.

6. John 15:15, emphasis added.

7. See John 14:12.

8. Hebrews 11:6, NIV.

9. Romans 10:17.

10. See Matthew 17:19–20.

11. Matthew 26:53–54.

12. Matthew 3:17; see also Matthew 12:18.

13. Matthew 4:1, NCV.

14. Luke 22:31, NCV.

CHAPTER 8: I HEAR THE VOICE OF THE FATHER

1. John 18:37.

2. Exodus 15:26, emphasis added.

3. Deuteronomy 28:2.

4. Deuteronomy 26:14.

5. Jeremiah 42:6.

6. John 6:45.

7. John 8:47, NIV.

8. Luke 11:28, NIV.

9. Henry T. Blackaby, *Experiencing God* (Nashville: Broadman and Holman Publishers, 2004), 137.

10. Hebrews 11:6, NIV.

11. Romans 10:17.

12. Revelation 3:22, NIV.

13. Job 33:14.

14. Blackaby, *Experiencing God*, 142.

15. 1 Samuel 16:7.

16. John 16:13.

17. James 1:2–4, NLT, emphasis added.

18. See John 10:10.

19. See Ephesians 6:13.

20. 1 Thessalonians 1:6, NLT.

21. 1 Thessalonians 2:18, NLT.

22. Jeremiah 2:19, NIV.

CHAPTER 9: HE KNEW HIS MISSION

1. John 17:18, THE MESSAGE.
2. John 10:10.
3. John 14:6.
4. John 14:6.
5. John 18:37.
6. Luke 22:28–29, NCV.
7. 1 Timothy 2:6, NLT.
8. John 14:9.

CHAPTER 10: I KNOW MY MISSION

1. Acts 20:24, GW, emphasis added.
2. 2 Corinthians 11:3.
3. John 20:21.
4. Rob Wegner, "Stories of 'Missional' in Real Life," *Outreach*, December 19, 2011, http://www.outreachmagazine.com/features/4520-Stories-Missional-Real-Life.html (accessed September 25, 2012).
5. 1 Corinthians 6:19–20, NAS.
6. John 14:15, NAS.
7. John 17:16, 18.
8. John 6:44.

PART 3: CRAVEABLE LOOKING

1. 2 Chronicles 16:9, NLT.
2. Jack Bechta, "Scouting Departments Are the R&D Arms of an NFL Team," NationalFootballPost.com, April 12, 2011, http://www.nationalfootballpost.com/Are-NFL-scouting-departments-underfunded.html (accessed September 25, 2012).
3. See 1 Samuel 16:1–13 for the whole story.

CHAPTER 11: HIS "ME" BECAME GOD'S "ME"

1. Hebrews 5:8, THE MESSAGE.
2. John 5:30, NIV.
3. Hebrews 4:15, NIV.
4. Matthew 26:39, GW.
5. Philippians 2:7, GW.
6. Jeremiah 29:11, NLT.
7. In John 7:37–39 Jesus described a believer as a person that "…out of his heart will flow rivers of living water" (v. 38, ESV). John identifies the "living water" as the "Spirit" in the passage. In Joel 2:28 God promised, "I will *pour* out my Spirit on all flesh" (ESV); this promise was quoted by Peter on the Day of Pentecost in Acts 2:17. Isaiah 44:3 made a direct comparison between water and the Spirit.
8. Luke 22:42, NLT.
9. Matthew 24:14.

CHAPTER 12: MY "ME" BECOMES GOD'S "ME"

1. 1 Corinthians 12:27, THE MESSAGE.
2. E. G. Carré, ed., *Praying Hyde, Apostle of Prayer: The Life Story of John Hyde* (Alachua, FL: Bridge-Logos, 1982), 40.
3. Luke 1:46.
4. Luke 17:21.
5. See Matthew 25:14–30 for the whole story.
6. Luke 17:11.
7. See Galatians 5:16.
8. Romans 8:5–8, NIV.
9. Matthew 10:38, NLT.
10. Hebrews 12:2.
11. See Galatians 5:16.
12. Romans 8:14, NIV.

CHAPTER 13: HE LOOKED FOR HIS "WE"

1. Luke 6:13.
2. John 6:44.
3. Luke 6:12–13.
4. See John 14:31.
5. Acts 16:6–7.
6. Acts 16:14.
7. 1 Corinthians 2:12.
8. 1 Corinthians 11:1, NIV.
9. 1 Corinthians 11:1.
10. Acts 20:25–27, NIV.
11. John 17:6.
12. Proverbs 11:25, NIV.
13. 1 John 2:6, THE MESSAGE.

CHAPTER 14: I LOOK FOR MY "WE"

1. Genesis 2:18.
2. Genesis 1:26, NIV.
3. John 5:30, NIV, emphasis added.
4. Gibbons, *Xealots*, 55.
5. John 13:35.
6. *Merriam-Webster's Collegiate Dictionary*, 11th edition (Springfield, MA: Merriam-Webster, Inc., 2003), s.v. "community."
7. 1 Thessalonians 2:8, NLT.
8. John 15:9, 12–13.
9. Hebrews 10:24–25, GNT.
10. Acts 2:47, GW.
11. John 13:34–35.
12. Galatians 6:2, NIV.

CHAPTER 15: HE LOOKED FOR HIS "US"

1. Mark 15:40–41, HCSB.

2. Matthew 11:28, NLT, emphasis added.

Chapter 16: I Look for My "Us"

1. Matthew 16:18, NLT.
2. Ephesians 4:11–12, NLT.
3. Ephesians 4:13, NLT.
4. 1 Corinthians 12:25, The Message.
5. Acts 2:46, GW.
6. Matthew 12:25, HCSB.
7. Acts 2:46–47, GW.
8. Mark Driscoll and Gerry Breshears, *Doctrine* (Wheaton, IL: Crossway, 2010), 307.
9. 1 Timothy 3:15, NLT.
10. Colossians 4:11, NLT.

Part 4: Craveable Loving

1. Mark 10:21.
2. Romans 1:28–32, emphasis added.

Chapter 17: He Loved "Out of Bounds"

1. Acts 10:28, NLT.
2. Matthew 11:19, NLV.
3. Proverbs 17:17.
4. See Matthew 9:12.
5. Luke 19:10.
6. 1 Corinthians 5:9–10.

1. Chapter 18: I Love "Out of Bounds" Luke 6:32, The Message.
2. Richard Beck, "The Bait and Switch of Contemporary Christianity," *God's Politics* (blog), Sojo.net, December 27, 2011, http://sojo.net/blogs/2011/12/27/bait-and-switch-contemporary-christianity (accessed October 1, 2012).
3. Luke 19:10.

Part 5: Craveable Living

1. James 1:23–24, The Message.
2. Psalm 90:12, NLT.

Chapter 19: He Demonstrated the Power of God

1. Matthew 13:54, GW.
2. Acts 8:19–20, NLT.
3. John 17:6.
4. John 4:48, NCV.
5. John 2:8–10.
6. John 2:11.
7. John 9:1–4, 7, 33, 35–38.
8. John 11:4, 41–46.
9. Luke 10:8–11.
10. John 2:23.
11. John 20:30–31.

12. John 10:38.

CHAPTER 20: I DEMONSTRATE THE POWER OF GOD

1. 1 Thessalonians 1:5, NLT.

2. Derwin Gray, "My Church Model Is Better Than Yours," "*Just Marinating*" (blog), January 12, 2012, http://www.derwinlgray.com/2012/01/page/4/ (accessed October 1, 2012).

3. John 10:37–38.

4. Acts 16:30, ESV.

5. 1 Corinthians 4:20.

6. Romans 8:19, HCSB.

7. Oswald Chambers, *My Utmost for His Highest* (Uhrichsville, OH: Barbour Publishing, Inc., 1935, 1963, 2000), September 20, "The Divine Rule of Life."

8. 1 Corinthians 2:1.

9. 1 Thessalonians 1:5, NCV.

CHAPTER 21: HE COMMUNICATED THE PURPOSE OF GOD

1. John 14:10.

2. John 8:31–32, ESV.

3. 2 Corinthians 5:5, NIV.

4. 2 Corinthians 3:18, NIV.

5. John 14:24, NIV.

6. Matthew 11:29, NLT.

7. 2 Corinthians 4:16.

8. 2 Corinthians 4:17–18, NIV.

9. John 6:63.

10. Psalm 138:8, NIV.

11. Isaiah 46:11.

CHAPTER 22: I COMMUNICATE THE PURPOSE OF GOD

1. 1 Corinthians 2:4–5, YLT.

2. Acts 1:6.

3. See Revelation 21 for a description of Jesus's eternal kingdom.

4. Philippians 2:10–11, ESV.

5. Rick Renner, *Sparkling Gems From the Greek* (Tulsa, OK: Teach All Nations, 2003), 359.

6. John 12:49.

7. Colossians 4:6, NLT.

8. John 4:26.

9. John 4:28–30, THE MESSAGE.

10. Matthew 7:6.

CHAPTER 23: HE IMITATED THE PERSON OF GOD

1. John 10:37.

2. John 14:9, THE MESSAGE.

3. John 8:58, ESV.

4. Philippians 2:5, NLT.

CHAPTER 24: I IMITATE THE PERSON OF GOD

1. Matthew 5:44–45.
2. Matthew 5:43–48.
3. See Romans 5:8.
4. Matthew 5:48.
5. Luke 15:1, THE MESSAGE.
6. Proverbs 19:6, NLT.
7. Artie Davis, "5 Traits of the Craveable," *Leading Big* (blog), September 27, 2012, http://artiedavis.com/2012/09/27/5-traits-of-the-craveable/ (accessed October 2, 2012).

PART 6: CRAVEABLE LEARNING

1. BrainyQuote.com, "Harold Wilson Quotes," http://www.brainyquote .com/quotes/quotes/h/haroldwils104500.html (accessed October 16, 2012).

CHAPTER 25: HE KNEW HOW TO GET THINGS DONE

1. Mark 2:17, THE MESSAGE.
2. 2 Samuel 22:31.
3. Ecclesiastes 11:5, NIV.
4. John 5:19–20.

CHAPTER 26: I KNOW HOW TO GET THINGS DONE

1. Exodus 4:12, NLT.
2. Ephesians 5:25, ESV.

CHAPTER 27: I KNOW HOW TO GET THINGS DONE NOW

1. 1 John 2:20.
2. Matthew 4:4.
3. 2 Corinthians 3:18, emphasis added.
4. 2 Timothy 3:16, NLT, emphasis added.
5. Psalm 37:23.
6. Proverbs 16:9.
7. Isaiah 37:26, NLT.

PART 7: CRAVEABLE LEADING

1. John 17:20–21.
2. See Genesis 3.
3. TwitterCounter.com, "The Top 100 Most Followed on Twitter," http:// twittercounter.com/pages/100 (accessed January 25, 2012). The number of followers have increased during the publication process of the book, but the rankings remain pretty consistent.
4. Pew Forum on Religion and Public Life, "A Report on the Size and Distribution of the World's Christian Population," December 19, 2011, http://www .pewforum.org/Christian/Global-Christianity-exec.aspx (accessed October 2, 2012).
5. John 1:1–5.

CHAPTER 28: HE LED OTHERS TO GET IN

1. John 14:12, NLT.

2. Mark 10:22, ESV.

3. Matthew 27:5, ESV.

4. Matthew 13:58, ESV.

5. John 7:52, ESV.

6. See John 19:25–27 for the story of Jesus's most loyal supporters, including His mother.

CHAPTER 29: I LEAD OTHERS TO GET IN

1. 1 Thessalonians 1:5–6.

2. Francis Chan, *Forgotten God* (Colorado Springs, CO: David C. Cook, 2009), 142.

3. James 2:22–23.

4. Romans 10:17.

5. Colossians 3:17, ESV.

6. 2 Corinthians 5:20, GW.

7. John 14:14, NAS.

8. Numbers 23:19.

9. Acts 8:4–8.

10. John 13:15, emphasis added.

11. Genesis 1:28.

12. Acts 9:31.

13. Luke 6:39–40.

14. Romans 1:14, NLV.

15. John 6:24, ERV, emphasis added.

CHAPTER 30: HE LED OTHERS TO GROW UP

1. 1 Thessalonians 3:2, GW.

2. Luke 2:52.

3. 2 Timothy 1:9, GW.

4. Luke 13:32–33, NAS.

5. Acts 1:8.

6. John 14:9, THE MESSAGE.

7. Luke 6:40, NCV.

8. John 14:11–13, NCV.

CHAPTER 31: I LEAD OTHERS TO GROW UP

1. Ephesians 4:15, ESV.

2. Genesis 12:1, NIV.

3. Genesis 12:9.

4. See Genesis 15:5–6.

5. Matthew 16:24, ESV.

CHAPTER 32: HE LED OTHERS TO GO OUT

1. John 17:18.

2. John 8:29.

3. Mark 3:14–15, NIV.

4. Mark 1:17.

5. Luke 4:43.

CHAPTER 33: I LEAD OTHERS TO GO OUT

1. Joshua 1:13–15.
2. Matthew 28:19, NCV.
3. Mark 3:13–15.
4. Acts 11:21, GW.

PART 8: CRAVEABLE LEAVING

1. John 3:16.

CHAPTER 34: HE LEFT A LEGACY

1. John 17:20–21, NLT.
2. TheFreeDictionary.com, s.v. "legacy," http://www.thefreedictionary.com/legacy (accessed October 2, 2012).
3. Luke 22:42, ESV.
4. Hebrews 4:15, ESV.
5. John 15:13, ESV.
6. Luke 6:40.
7. Mark 1:38, NCV.

CHAPTER 35: I LEAVE A LEGACY

1. John 17:4, NIV.
2. John 21:18–19, GW..
3. Acts 26:15–16.
4. 2 Corinthians 3:5–6, NAS.
5. Deuteronomy 10:11.
6. 2 Thessalonians 1:11, NLT.
7. Titus 2:12, NLT.
8. Colossians 1:5–6, ESV, emphasis added.
9. 1 John 2:6, emphasis added.

PART 9: CRAVEABLE US

1. Romans 14:17, NIV.

CHAPTER 36: THE CULTURE MATTERS

1. 1 Corinthians 9:22–23.
2. Merriam-Webster.com, "s.v. culture," http://www.merriam-webster.com/dictionary/culture (accessed October 3, 2012).
3. Philippians 2:14, NCV.
4. 1 Corinthians 9:19–23, THE MESSAGE.
5. Acts 16:1–3.
6. John 6:68, ESV.

CHAPTER 37: THE CITY MATTERS

1. Galatians 3:28, NIV.
2. Acts 8:4–8.
3. 1 Corinthians 6:9–11, NIV.
4. Romans 5:8.
5. Romans 5:7–8, NIV.

CHAPTER 38: THE CROWD MATTERS

1. Matthew 5:16, THE MESSAGE.
2. Luke 19:1–10.
3. Matthew 9:20–22.
4. Colossians 4:5, NLT.
5. Philemon 6.
6. Titus 2:10, NLT.

CHAPTER 39: THE CHURCH MATTERS

1. Acts 2:47.
2. Genesis 11:6, NLT.
3. Acts 9:31.
4. Acts 4:30–31.
5. Acts 8:9, 13.
6. Acts 2:2–4, NCV.
7. 1 Kings 3:3, ESV.
8. See 1 Kings 3:7.
9. 1 Kings 3:9, ESV.
10. John 14:34–35.

CHAPTER 40: THE CIRCLE MATTERS

1. Proverbs 27:17.
2. As quoted in "Why Can I Only Share With 150 People?", Path.com, July 19, 2012, http://service.path.com/customer/portal/articles/257552-why-can-i -only-share-with-15-people (accessed October 3, 2012).
3. Numbers 14:9, ESV.
4. See Deuteronomy 11:23–24; Joshua 1:3.
5. See John 14:12.
6. See Matthew 14:22–33.
7. Colossians 4:11, NLT.